ALONG THE
YORKSHIRE
COAST

THE TEES TO THE HUMBER

Along the
Yorkshire
Coast

From the Tees to the Humber

David Brandon

First published 2010

The History Press
The Mill, Brimscombe Port
Stroud, Gloucestershire, GL5 2QG
www.thehistorypress.co.uk

British Library Cataloguing in Publication Data.
A catalogue record for this book is available from the British Library.

ISBN 978 0 7524 5732 1

Typesetting and origination by The History Press
Printed in Great Britain
Manufacturing managed by Jellyfish Print Solutions Ltd

CONTENTS

I

THE COAST – A CONSTANT BATTLEGROUND

Acoastline is where two very different worlds meet and confront each other – the land and the sea. The confrontation can be violent; land is pounded and destroyed at one point, but in doing that, the sea causes land to be built elsewhere. This seemingly contradictory phenomenon is readily evident along the Yorkshire coast. The coast can offer the dramatic sight and sound of enormous waves pounding tall cliffs with immense force one day, only to be followed the next day at the same place by tiny wavelets lapping the sandy beach. Even low-lying and normally peaceful-looking littoral areas, such as the coast south of Bridlington, can be transformed dramatically into a battleground between land and sea which possesses a forcefulness and violence beyond human control. This was demonstrated so effectively and frighteningly in the east coast surge of 1953.

The coast can also be described as a world in its own right. It has its own specialised wildlife, such as cliff-nesting birds, waders, inshore fish, crustaceans, invertebrates, seaweeds and land plants with a high tolerance for salt. The coastline also has its own specialised human community of those who have chosen to use the sea and extract their livelihoods from it. It could be said that mariners and fisherfolk are engaged in a permanent battle with that unpredictable, highly-demanding, dangerous and often treacherous element. Other people, such as those in the leisure and hospitality industries, obtain their living from servicing the needs of those who are drawn to the coast for the purposes of pleasure and recreation. The relationship between man and the sea is a complex one, seemingly unchanging in respect of certain constants and yet, like all historical phenomena, undergoing a process of continuous evolution.

Just as human society is in a constant state of flux, so too is the coastline. For most of the time this movement is too slow for us to notice the changes. The Yorkshire coast has, however, provided definite and even spectacular evidence of change in our lifetimes. The sea constantly batters and disintegrates a headland here and scours out a bay there, carrying the eroded debris away and often dumping it down the coast in the form of a sand bar, a spit or as muddy saltings. The buildings erected by humans are seen for the puny efforts they are when the sea decides to subsume them into its hungry maw.

There are three main ways in which the waves erode the land mass. The first is corrosion. Sea water near the coast usually has tiny particles of rock in suspension and these have some corroding effect even in gentle sea conditions. The corrosive effect of the material in suspension is obviously concentrated on the base of the cliffs. Here a notch is gradually carved which undercuts the face of the cliff. The overhanging rock is subject to attack by the freezing and thawing of water trapped in crevices, as well as by other erosive action, and eventually the force of gravity may become too much and a section of the cliff will fall. Under storm conditions, however, the tidal surges can be sufficiently powerful to carry cobbles, pebbles and boulders and hurl them bodily at the cliffs.

The second form of wave action is quite different and operates through hydraulic principles. When a wave, especially a powerful one, strikes a cliff, any pockets of air which are trapped in crevices are compressed. A split second later as the wave retreats, the compressed air expands again only for another wave to arrive immediately. This repeated compression and expansion of air exerts a great strain on the fabric of the cliff face, causing fissures to widen until a flake, a sliver, or perhaps a slab of rock, is in effect blasted away.

The third form of wave action is perhaps more insidious and erosive, being of a chemical nature. Sea water contains salts which are particularly damaging to rocks of an alkaline constitution (chalk and limestone in particular) and it dissolves them and carries its spoils away in suspension.

Cliffs may contain strata of various kinds of rock whose properties are very different and that either withstand or succumb to these attacks in different ways. Sometimes the strata are horizontal but they may be inclined, even vertical, where they outcrop in the cliff face. Tough rocks may be more resistant but they can themselves become weakened if softer rocks near them break and fall. Caves sometimes form where waves assault a weak point at the base of a cliff. This could be in a patch of softer rock or a spot where joints or a fault reduce the power of the rock to resist assault. Flamborough Head provides some very fine examples of this kind of cliff. In one place there is a blow-hole or 'gloup' formed where the sea's blasting has undermined part of a cave roof, allowing waves to gush up through a fissure in the rock and shoot spectacularly into the air above. The point about all this is that nothing is static; where sea meets land a remorseless struggle is taking place all the time. However, what the sea takes away from one place, it tends to deposit somewhere else.

The rate at which the sea advances against the land is influenced by the inter-relationship between various factors. One might expect that the western coasts of Britain, being so exposed to the prevailing westerly winds and bearing the full force of Atlantic storms, would be retreating much more swiftly than the relatively more sheltered shores of the North Sea. In fact, the reverse is true. This is largely because the west coasts are guarded by buttresses of tough old rock while those of the east coast are composed predominantly of soft chalk, young limestone and sandstone, and newer, soft, unconsolidated clays. ('Young' and 'new' are used in the geological sense.)

Some of the most dramatic rates of marine erosion are actually to be found in the cliffs formed of glacial boulder clay in the Holderness region of the Yorkshire coast. Here the coastal strip is retreating at an average of two yards a year. Since the start of the Middle Ages, at least two dozen villages and hamlets have been lost to the sea in the area between Flamborough Head and Spurn Point. It is estimated that a tract of land of about 80 square miles, to the south of Bridlington, has disappeared into the sea since Roman times. We should of course remember that the east and south-east of Britain is slowly sinking anyway, exacerbating the effects mentioned.

Local artists and photographers have provided graphic pictures of churches poised precariously on the tops of cliffs at the base of which huge waves are battering. An example is Kilnsea. This is where the boulder clay of Holderness gives way to the narrow neck of sand ending in Spurn Point. Here the parish church was still on the top of the low cliff in 1826 but everyone was aware its days were numbered. Everyone was aware that its days were numbered. The last burial in the churchyard took place in 1823 and it was wisely decided to close the church for worship in late 1824, just before the winter storms were expected. Less than ten years later, not only the church but most of the nearby houses had disappeared into the sea. The church went, with a tremendous crash and surprising completeness, one night in the autumn of 1830. The few dwellings which currently make up Kilnsea were well inland at the time. They are now not far from the sea.

After the 1953 floods, a stretch of the shore at Kilnsea was given sea defences in the form of a concrete promenade, groynes and a stone facing to the clay cliffs. Within twenty years the whole structure had been reduced to rubble. It is not just that mankind is incompetent or incapable in his attempts to staunch the power of the sea. Here the boulder clay, which is alternately wetted and then dried out, starts to crumble and with heavy rain easily turns into mud slides. Except for larger settlements like Hornsea and Withernsea, the cost of further

The parish church at Kilnsea before it went over the cliffs in 1830.

coastal defences simply cannot be justified and more buildings will undoubtedly be seized by the sea over the next few years. Few coastlines anywhere in the world are eroding as quickly as that of Holderness.

In the geological short term, much of the eroded material will go to form beaches close to or sometimes rather more distant from where it originated. In longer geological terms, this material will be compacted into new rocks as the great cycle of building and breaking and transportation rolls on.

The eroded material is moved up the beach in the swash of the waves and then seaward again by the backwash. However, since waves normally approach the land at an oblique angle, the material is also moved along the shore. This phenomenon is known as longshore drift. It means that some material may travel considerable distances along the coast or find itself in stretches of sand which dry out and are blown inland or elsewhere. Many readers have probably seen or felt the mini-sandstorms that occur on the exposed beach at Skegness in Lincolnshire.

The Yorkshire coast has a very fine example of the phenomenon known as a spit: Spurn Head. Spits are attached to the land and composed largely of material scoured and transported from beaches elsewhere and also deposited by rivers. (Spits are small tails of sand or shingle attached to the shore and they gradually lengthen, sometimes running parallel to the coast. They continue to grow until they reach water which is deep enough to permit fierce wave action.)

This view of the lighthouse at Spurn Head gives an idea of the bleak, open and vulnerable nature of the coast at this point.

In the case of Spurn Head, material drifting southwards down the east coast meets different kinds of material being brought down by the mighty Humber which slows as it approaches the sea. Being slower, the water cannot carry so much material in suspension and much is dropped where it meets the force of the sea. The sea, equally, dumps much of its material in suspension where it meets the force of the out-flowing Humber. This low-lying bank of sand and shingle is a natural battleground between the forces of erosion and deposition. From time to time, especially as the result of extreme storms, the spit breaks and an island is created. Over time the new island is washed away and the spit continues growing in a south-westerly direction.

The Case of Ravenser Odd

Few people have heard of Ravenser Odd. For some time in the Middle Ages, probably from around 1250, it was an important port. It was on a small island formed from the spit and not far from where Spurn Head then was. No trace of it now exists and research has not even managed to identify the exact spot where it stood. What is the reason for its disappearance? The sea.

The coast of Holderness is very unstable, being under constant erosive attack not only by the North Sea but also from the waters of the Humber. The coast of east Yorkshire once ran further west, following a chalk cliff from Hessle on the Humber via Beverley to Flamborough. The low-lying land that is now Holderness was a shallow bay of the sea. About 2 million years ago, glaciers coming from the north covered this area and, when they later retreated, they left behind that collection of detritus known as boulder clay, consisting of errant rocks, mud and gravel. These filled up the area where the bay had been and created the fertile but flat land that came to be known as Holderness.

Close to Ravenser Odd was the port of Ravenser, which was probably the place from which what was left of the invading army of Harald Hardrada, the King of Norway, set sail for home. (This army had been severely defeated in 1066 by King Harold of England at the Battle of Stamford Bridge, near York.) It is thought that Ravenser and Ravenser Odd were joined by some kind of causeway similar to that between the coast of Northumberland and the island of Lindisfarne. (It is all rather confusing for historians because sometimes Ravenser and Ravenser Odd are mentioned almost as if they are one and the same place.)

The records strongly suggest that Ravenser Odd in the 1240s had the status of a borough and therefore boasted a mayor, burgesses, a court and various privileges. In 1251 its status was such that it had a weekly market and an annual fair, and was a town of real significance. In 1347 it is thought to have had something like 300 buildings. Even before that, the town had two MPs. Its significance was recognised by its having to meet royal demands to supply ships and men for naval purposes. Its growth as a port was assisted by its being directly on the sea, as opposed to both Hull and Grimsby which were several miles upriver.

However, Ravenser Odd suffered a number of incursions from the sea and by the 1340s the place was in serious danger of being destroyed as sea levels rose. Most of the inhabitants had moved out and the settlement went into very rapid decline. Those few inhabitants who remained were horrified in 1355 when the tides began exhuming bodies from the churchyard.

To prevent this happening again, the remaining bodies were disinterred and reburied at Easington, nearby. By the end of the fourteenth century, Ravenser Odd had virtually disappeared and all that was left of Ravenser was its manor house. The townsfolk, or what was left of them, decamped, mostly to go to Hull.

Similar problems occurred a few miles west on the north bank of the Humber Estuary. In the twelfth and thirteenth centuries, considerable land reclamation had taken place in this area, much of it the work of the Cistercian monks of Meaux Abbey nearby. The site is about 6 miles north of Hull and there is little to see today because most of the fabric was dismantled and taken away to be used by the King in building the defences of Hull. This reclamation meant the northern shores of the Humber are about 2 miles further south today. The land was used as pasture for sheep grazing. Two substantial villages existed by the names of Sunthorp and Orwithfleet. Little more is known about them.

The existence and subsequent disappearance of human settlements in such a relatively short time is evidence of the to and fro of the relationship between man and the sea. It also adds enormously to the mystique of this remote and largely unvisited part of Britain.

2

THE NORTH SEA

It is impossible to think of the Yorkshire coast without thinking of the North Sea, or 'German Ocean' as it was often referred to. The history of the people who have lived along this coast has been enormously influenced by, and interlinked with, its massive presence. Here we look briefly at its history, the invaders who crossed it, the trading links that have been forged with the countries that border it and the role it has played in Britain's mercantile and naval development.

At one time the North Sea was an inland lake as land bridges linked what became Britain with Scandinavia and Western Europe. Later on, around 300,000 years ago, most of it was covered in a polar ice sheet. About 7,500 years ago the Straits of Dover were breached and the North Sea grew considerably in size, much of its southern parts having previously been dry land. One feature of the North Sea is the fact that it is shallow. Going northwards, only when the Shetland Islands are reached does it exceed a depth of 100 fathoms and the area of the Dogger Bank is particularly shallow.

The shape of the North Sea has made it prone to disasters. When the Atlantic Ocean is experiencing severe weather conditions, and these are combined with high spring tides, the funnel-shape of the North Sea means that overspill is likely to flood low-lying parts of its shores. The worst such disaster in living memory was of course in 1953.

The North Sea has been the route by which many invaders have arrived on these shores. Some came as raiders, who plundered easily accessible settlements and then headed back across the sea with their bounty. Others must have liked what they saw and they decided to settle. In doing so, they radically changed existing patterns of culture. Very significant Germanic and Nordic elements took root and in so doing tended to push the Celtic elements of the population to the further fringes of the British Isles.

Attacks on the Yorkshire coast began while the Romans still occupied Britain and they proved as much of a nuisance here as other raiders did on the European Continent, chipping away at the beleaguered Roman Empire. Invaders included Saxons, Angles and Jutes. Those that settled took to farming and, in due course, they themselves were raided and later invaded.

The Vikings and the Norsemen came to this coast as pirates and plunderers who employed a kind of blitzkrieg. They appeared over the horizon, ran their ships up the beach or penetrated far up navigable rivers, dashed to any places that looked as if they might have worthwhile booty, grabbed anything valuable and portable, put anybody who got in the way to the sword, usually set fire to anything easily flammable and then disappeared from whence they had come. They were not Christians so churches and other religious buildings were fair game. They and their vessels looked terrifying and the speed with which they carried out these sorties meant that the locals were left with little time to secrete either their valuables or themselves. They seem to have had a particular penchant for grabbing and carrying off comely local wenches.

Over time, what were purely raiding sorties changed into settlement. They tended to find an easily defensible position near navigable water, fortify it, and then use it as a base from which to plunder the surrounding countryside and either kill or browbeat the inhabitants into submission. For men who mastered ships and the seas in the way they did, it is also remarkable that in land warfare they made extensive and very successful use of horses. However, they weren't averse to being bought off. After all, taking tribute in the form of Danegeld from the locals was less effort, although admittedly not as exciting as beating them to a pulp. The trouble from the point of view of the locals of paying Danegeld was that, like most forms of extortion, the price being demanded constantly increased.

The invasions of Britain by the Romans, Anglo-Saxons, Danes and Normans all served to build trading and commerce links with the countries of the Continent. Much of this was across the North Sea. We know that York in the tenth century had a thriving colony of Danes engaged in commercial activity, and that much of their business was waterborne from Scandinavia across the North Sea to the Humber and then up the Yorkshire Ouse, and vice versa. One commodity which we know they traded in was English woollen cloth. Other products likely to have been exported were grain, wool, hides and animals skins and possibly coal. An interesting export was that of grindstones made from the aptly-named millstone grit of the Pennines. It has to be said that the only consistently significant trading port of the Yorkshire coast in the Middle Ages was Hull, but it was never the equal of the East Anglian ports of Boston, Lynn, Yarmouth and Ipswich.

The development of trading relations inevitably meant that foreigners from the countries involved settled in this country, especially in Hull, albeit not in very large numbers. This is hardly surprising because they seem to have had a fairly hostile reception from the native English. Regarded as aliens, they were subjected to official discrimination. They were made the subject of extra taxes from time to time and it was rare for them, for example, to be allowed legal redress in the courts. On a personal basis they usually met with varying degrees of hostility but assimilated happily enough after a generation or two. The Flemings were singled out for mockery on account of what was generally regarded as their uncouth behaviour. Whether foreigners in England were treated any worse than English people who settled overseas is a matter for conjecture, although Britain's island position may have encouraged in its inhabitants an extra degree of xenophobia.

One area in which England was more progressive than France, for example, was in its social structure, which had no legal or other barriers to prevent members of the merchant class from rising to positions not only of enormous wealth and power but also of status and prestige. A very good example was the de la Pole family of Hull. Long-standing inhabitants of the town, they owed their rise to William de la Pole, who conducted a number of very successful money-making enterprises for Edward III. The King gave him several very responsible missions to conduct on his behalf both at home and abroad, which he carried out with great skill and diplomacy. He was knighted and rose to a position of great prominence in the Court. He was regarded as a parvenu,by older-established feudal barons but this does not seem to have affected his ascending career.

In the middle of the fourteenth century, the Hanseatic League, also known as the Hansa, had profound influence on the east coast ports. The Hansa was a confederation of north German and Baltic seaports intended to cut out wasteful competition and to have the strength resulting from their combined power to dominate and almost monopolise trade and commerce on the Baltic and North Seas. It had what might be described as outposts in England, including one at Hull and another at York. The Hansa became powerful enough to operate economic sanctions and even take naval action on those occasions when its position was challenged. Although the Hansa was never omnipotent, it was certainly strong enough to limit English trading on the other side of the North Sea. The Hansa only really went into decline during the reign of Elizabeth I, once England was beginning to enrich herself by exploration and opening up new trade relationships with the Americas and the Orient.

No sooner was the Hanseatic League seen off in the sixteenth century than the London-based Company of Merchant Adventurers emerged. This received a royal charter awarding it the monopoly of trade, except that in wool, with the Low Countries and Germany. In return for this monopoly, the Merchant Adventurers gave a share of their proceeds to the Crown. There was a great deal of animosity to this development and we know that in the middle of the sixteenth century the merchants of York, Hull and Newcastle petitioned the Crown in an attempt to win what would now be called a level playing field. They were unsuccessful. Elizabeth found the Company a more than useful source of income. In the event, it was not until the late seventeenth century that the influence of the Merchant Adventurers was seriously undermined.

Even in the Middle Ages, the Yorkshire coast remained very vulnerable to seaborne malefactors. Pirates from the Low Countries, Germany, Spain, Scotland and also other parts of England operated with almost total impunity, capturing ocean-going and coastal shipping and sometimes raiding coastal communities. It should be remembered that there was no concept of a permanent navy until Tudor times and no standing army.

Fishing in the North Sea

Evidence has been found that the Romans fished at sea during their occupation of England and that the Vikings were fine navigators and fishermen. They were particularly partial to herrings. By the twelfth century, boats from east coast ports were reaching the Iceland fishing grounds seeking white fish and especially cod.

It is hard for us in the twenty-first century to have any conception of how important herrings and salt cod, or stockfish as it was called, were to our medieval predecessors. The Church ordained the consumption of fish on many fasting days throughout the year. Both species existed in quantities to baffle the human imagination, yet from early times, English fisherfolk were engaged in unfriendly fishing rivalry, particularly with the Dutch. For whatever reasons, the English always seemed to lag behind the Dutch in the quality and durability of their fishing boats and in the skill with which they salted and pickled the fish they caught. The presence of the Dutch fishing off the Yorkshire coast was something that was greatly resented. by the English. In 1394, for example, Richard II ordered the magistrates of Whitby to prohibit foreigners bringing catches of herrings into that town for sale. Occasionally Dutch ships, men or their catches would be seized by the English and then the Dutch would take reprisals in a kind of rehearsal for the so-called 'Cod Wars' of more recent years.

The area of the North Sea lying between the Dogger Bank, the Silver Pits and the Yorkshire coast was perhaps the most productive of all the fishing grounds surrounding the British Isles. From the sixteenth to the nineteenth centuries, each year between March and October, this area was intensively fished by Yorkshiremen from the various seaside settlements. In 1800 a typical example of their vessels would have been around 58 tons, clinker-built and about 40-50ft long and 17ft in the beam. It would be three-masted and contain a crew of seven. Five of them would constitute the crew and they would all have a share in the boat and its equipment. There would also be a cook, who had a half-share, and a boy, who received a small wage. They would be accompanied by smaller vessels of the sort we now tend to call 'cobles'. Modern examples of these tough, flat-bottomed little boats can still be seen in substantial

Hull's Maritime Museum contains many models of the various types of craft that plied the waters off the Yorkshire coast.

numbers along the Yorkshire coast. Cobles are almost certainly Scandinavian in origin and they owe their sharply-pointed prow and stern to the requirement that they could be launched from the beach and manoeuvred either forwards or backwards in the turbulent seas which are so much a feature of this coast.

Since most of the fishing was carried out by hook and line, plentiful supplies of bait were needed before setting off for sea. This was the responsibility of the womenfolk. The 'flither-girls' collected mussels preferably, or limpets, in vast quantities. These, together with crabs and sand eels, were used to bait the lines, or 'scane' them as they said in these parts. The lines were up to 400 yards long and furnished with anything between 280 and 400 hooks. Having set off on a Monday morning during the season, the boats arrived at the fishing grounds and dropped anchor. The cobles were about 25ft long and it was these which did the actual fishing. Twice a day, when the tide flowed and they were just a few miles offshore, they put out the lines. They caught great quantities of cod, ling, halibut, turbot, haddock, skate, whiting, sole, plaice, flounder and dab, for example. These were transferred to the five-man boat. After three or four days fishing, the entourage headed back home where hopefully the catch would be sold, the profits and wages taken out and preparations made for the next week's fishing expedition.

It is often not realised by those used to consuming fish and chips that the cod can be a very large fish, more than 2m in length and weighing as much as 90kg, about 200lbs. Other members of the Gadidae family include haddock, hake, ling, saithe and whiting. The post-war generation of British children grew up with cod liver oil, the health-giving properties of which were considered second to none. Its use assured extra demand for cod, which was good for the fishing industry.

Until the late eighteenth century, Yorkshire's fishing industry was largely inshore and small-scale, working out of the various coastal communities and doing little more than supplying local demand. Fish were caught by gill nets and hook and line. However, from the 1830s larger boats called drifters came into use and they began to transform the industry using trawl-gear which was dragged along the sea bed and provided the opportunity to seize much larger catches. This also enabled demersal fish like sole, turbot and brill to be snaffled up. Unfortunately, at this time the huge nets used were indiscriminate about the size of the fish they caught and many fish too small to be much use for the market were caught, thereby threatening future stocks.

The industry began to be much more capital-intensive and with the development of railways it was completely transformed. Fish is very perishable but it could now be iced and moved swiftly by fast trains to the inland centres of population, and most of all to the huge London market at Billingsgate. The availability of fresh fish at an affordable price effected a remarkable improvement in the diet of the urban working classes. The herring in particular became the traditional food of the poor and, at least when the season was on, they were extremely cheap.

Grimsby (which is northern Lincolnshire but on the south bank of the Humber), serves as an example. Of all the places that became major fishing ports in the nineteenth century consequent on the building of the railways, the archetype was Grimsby. Ice was imported in vast amounts from Norway. From 1850 steam-powered trawlers began to come into service. Steam was not only used for propulsion but for powering the winches which made operating the nets so much easier. The rise of Grimsby is indicated by these figures: 453 tons landed in

1854; 1890, 70,000; 1900, 135,000 and 1958, 220,000 tons. Grimsby became the cutting-edge in all things to do with large-scale deep-sea fishing. A factory was established making artificial ice and soon trawlers were going to sea for long trips to distant and rich fishing grounds equipped in such a way that they could freeze their catch as they went. The vessels concerned tended not only to be steam-powered but also considerably larger. Operating them obviously needed massive financial investment. What was true of Grimsby was also true, only on a somewhat smaller scale, for Hull. It had 386 registered fishing vessels in 1876 and specialised in deep-sea trawling to destinations like Iceland and Newfoundland. As late as 1970, Hull had almost 300 trawlers. Even Scarborough had 123 registered vessels in 1876. The highly capitalised nature of the operations at such ports as these reduced operations elsewhere at smaller places to little more than inshore fishing largely for local demand and often for the holiday trade.

The major fishing ports of Grimsby and Hull, whose activities were heavily capitalised, developed what was known as the 'boxing' process in the middle of the nineteenth century for operations in the North Sea. This involved a high level of co-operation between individual owners. A fleet of smacks put to sea for up to eight weeks at a time and fed their catches into a carrier vessel (from the 1860s a steam trawler) which then whisked its perishable cargo off to market, often Billingsgate in London. This system continued in use until the 1930s. This was fishing on a truly industrial scale for the mass markets provided by the growing urban inland areas of Britain.

A famous feature of the herring industry was the migratory nature of the shoals which took several weeks to make their way down the east coast. The processing of the herrings was the prerogative of thousands of Scottish fisher-girls who followed the fish southwards. The word that comes to mind to describe these girls is 'robust' and certainly several hundred taking up temporary residence in a place like Whitby must have added something to the ambience and character of the place.

Yorkshire boats would take part in the few frenzied weeks of the herring fishery. Ten days fishing might net as many as 300,000 of what were known as the 'silver darlings'. Some of the catch would be smoked and kippered. They were cleaned and split and packed overnight in coarse-grained salt, the coarser the better, since it prevented the fish from lying too closely together. Next day long sticks were passed through where their eyes had been and, arranged in rows, they were hung from beams in specially-built smoke-houses where the fumes from smouldering oak chips slowly changed their colour from silver to burnished copper – hence the 'red herring'. There are still working smoke houses at Whitby.

The peak of the British herring industry was before the First World War when, one year, along the whole east coast, a scarcely believable 356 million tons of herrings was landed. The industry is now all but defunct. Fashions have changed and oily fish are no longer prized as much as they were, especially as their price has gone up. However, the culinary revolution of the last twenty years is recognising what marvellous meals can be made using herrings and also that more prolific, and somewhat despised, fish known as the mackerel.

There is still a lot of herring in the North Sea but the Germans and the Dutch catch most of it and it is used for fish meal and for various oil extracts. Most of the herring caught is immature and undersized, but size doesn't matter when the fish are being processed. This kind of fishing is often referred to as 'industrial fishing'.

Most of the settlements along the Yorkshire coast still have a few fishermen who go out for herrings, some white fish and shellfish. This part of the industry is small-scale, the fishermen may be part-time and the equipment needed is not prohibitively expensive. The results of their efforts can be seen every morning on the lively quays at Scarborough or Whitby, for example.

During the First World War, the fishermen of Yorkshire found themselves and their vessels commandeered for minesweeping duties which were especially hazardous. The reasoning of the Royal Navy was that fishermen already knew all about handling wires and trawls, fishing itself was virtually impossible during hostilities, and the men were familiar with the coast and the sea. A large number of mines were rendered harmless, however many fishing vessels fell foul of mines or attacks by enemy surface warships, submarines and aircraft, and many men died. It was the understated heroism of men in small boats for whom danger was a fact of life. Trawlers also acted as patrol vessels, convoy escorts and U-boat hunters. They were usually equipped with an antiquated gun and their record, while lacking the glamour of larger surface units, was one of which the survivors could justifiably be proud.

It is necessary to say something about the coasting trade. Before the building of the canals and the railways, rivers and the open sea provided the easiest way of transporting goods over longer distances and, for that reason, the coasting trade has existed since time immemorial. In the seventeenth century it was reckoned to be up to twenty times cheaper to send goods by water than by road. The stretch of coast that we are looking at has few rivers of any size except the Tees to the north and of course the mighty Humber into which flow several very important rivers that drain a fifth of the whole area of England, including the East Midlands and much of industrial Yorkshire.

The men who engaged in the coastal trade took part in a particularly hazardous calling. They were exposed to the attentions of pirates and enemy warships and had the additional hazards that arose from sailing close to the east coast. The North Sea's tidal ranges, hidden shoals and extreme changes of mood make it a killing ground for unwary, unlucky or incompetent seamen. The perceived hazards were such that the sturdy little collier ships that carried seacoal from the North-East to London usually did not venture to make the journey in December, January or February. Of course, many ships paid the price of defying the North Sea and a sailor in 1676 left a diary in which he declared, 'the sea is so full of wrecks on these coasts that those at sea are forced to look sharp to steer clear of them.' Many sailors preferred the more predictable hazards of a voyage to the East Indies to a winter journey down the east coast.

Over the centuries, navigation became somewhat safer. In early times, ships hugged the coast because they had few navigational aids. In fact, they sailed largely by sight and recognition of landmarks, and this meant sailing close to the shore with the attendant dangers involved in doing so. Sailing vessels were more difficult to handle and manoeuvre than steam ships. At night, sometimes the only means available to them to try to establish their whereabouts was by swinging the lead to find out the nature of the sea bottom. This required a minute knowledge of coastal conditions. Early charts were notoriously inaccurate.

Yorkshire was lucky in having a few places where ships could ride out a violent storm. Scarborough, Whitby and Bridlington provided relatively safe havens with their enclosed harbours, and levies were required from Tyne colliers and other vessels for the upkeep of the harbours of which they sometimes made extensive use. The Humber also made excellent shelter but, other than those places mentioned, the Yorkshire coast offered little cheer or comfort to ships in distress.

The number of vessels lost in the days before steam must have been staggering. One estimate gives a figure of over 50,000 ships wrecked on the Yorkshire coast since 1500. In the Middle Ages losses were numerous enough to make the Rights of Wreck among the most valuable of territorial privileges; in the Whitby area these were largely controlled by the abbey. People along the Yorkshire coast were always ready to exploit the misfortunes of distressed mariners and merchants to the full by mistreating the castaways and stealing the cargoes and even the fabric of their ships. Masts, spars, beams, planking and canvas all had use-value. Good pieces of timber went into the fabric of many a house along the coast. Lady Margaret Hoby, of the family who acquired the Rights of Wreck after Whitby Abbey was dissolved, wrote in her diary in 1603, 'This day it was told Mr Hoby that a ship was wrecked at Burniston upon his land and thus at all times God bestowed benefits on us. God make us thankful.' For the owners of the vessels concerned, after the pious words were spoken, the major concern has often been less about the fate of those on board and more about the financial investment involved in the ships themselves and their cargoes, and whether that investment can be recouped through insurance.

Losses of ships in the coasting trade were extensive at times of war both from privateers and warships. Sometimes merchant ships were requisitioned for naval use. One answer to the depredations caused by enemy ships was the convoy system with naval escorts. In 1666 many Newcastle colliers were detained in port for want of naval escorts and miners were being laid off as a consequence. Apparently a consortium of London brewers, who depended on coal for the production of beer, became so impatient that they hired armed vessels to escort Newcastle colliers southwards in direct defiance of Admiralty instructions. Those who owned coasting ships were often wary of forming up in convoys because the naval authorities often took the opportunity to pressgang experienced seamen. An order went out in 1653 that men aged forty and over, and young lads, were not to be forcibly taken off Newcastle colliers, but apparently this order was often observed in the breach.

The ships engaged in the coasting trade were of all shapes and sizes. There were small open sailing barges which ran short journeys between neighbouring ports; there were single-sailed square-rigged sloops that carried timber; and three-masted square riggers which handled most of the coal trade. The colliers, which were the largest vessels engaged in the east coast trade, did not exceed 400 tons. These highly specialised ships were toughly built to withstand the rigours of the North Sea and were designed to combine the ability to carry a heavy load with ease of handling in demanding conditions. The last of the shallow-draught sailing barges, incidentally, only went out of service in the 1950s. Not all the colliers took coal to London. Small vessels often ran up a Yorkshire beach at low tide and unloaded their coal into small horse-drawn carts, sometimes in turn taking on a cargo of alum or iron ore.

Only relatively small vessels are likely to have been built at any of the ports along the Yorkshire coast. The exception appears to have been Whitby, which certainly built colliers. Whitby might well have developed as a far greater commercial port and shipbuilding centre because of its exceptional harbour had it not had its problem of difficult communications inland. Scarborough also had a thriving shipbuilding industry.

If in the sixteenth century it was the Spanish that the British loved to hate, in the seventeenth especially and for much of the eighteenth, it was the Dutch. The wealth and power of Holland depended on her overseas trade and she became involved in overseas trading and the development of dominions before Britain did so. She also dominated the carrying trade and her ships were used by other nations to trade around the world, much to the chagrin of the British. Britain, which developed the same kind of interests under the Tudors but lagged significantly behind the Dutch, held one great trump card: control, at least in theory, of the English Channel through which Dutch ships had to pass as they went about their worldwide business. For that reason relations with the Dutch were fraught throughout this period and many battles were fought, mostly further south, over the issue of controlling the Channel. The set-piece actions tended to take place elsewhere, but inevitably hostilities spilt over to the Yorkshire coast and Dutch naval vessels, privateers and pirates randomly plundered British coastal and other shipping and from time to time raided coastal settlements. The British did the same to them. Sometimes we allied ourselves with the French against the Dutch but it was just as likely that we would briefly get together with the Dutch against the French. They would also sometimes unite against us. It was all very confusing.

3

MIDDLESBROUGH TO SANDSEND

This is a coastline of cliffs where the Cleveland Hills meet the sea. Many of the cliffs are quite spectacular and a rocky shoreline provides a superb setting for coastal walks. Streams run off the moors inland and have cut narrow, steep-sided valleys at the seaward end. Some of these have picturesque sheltered fishing villages. In 1974, Saltburn to Scalby Ness near Scarborough was designated a Heritage Coast. Along it runs part of the long-distance footpath, the Cleveland Way.

Middlesbrough

Middlesbrough is a product of the Industrial Revolution. It was no more than a tiny hamlet when, in 1830, an extension of the Stockton & Darlington Railway was opened for the purpose of carrying coal from South Durham to the navigable water of the River Tees at Stockton. The Pease Family, ubiquitous in these parts, bought about 500 acres of land and started the Owners of the Middlesbrough Estate to develop the site and open the docks, particularly for the export of coal. Middlesbrough became a boom town, expanding from a population of just forty in 1830 to 40,000 by 1870 and 90,000 by 1900. About 1850, iron ore was discovered in the Cleveland Hills and an iron and steel industry was established by Henry Bolckow and John Vaughan. Coal could be brought in very easily. The town went on to become the centre of a large and heavily industrialised conurbation including Stockton, Thornaby, Billingham, Norton, Ormesby and Grangetown. It became renowned for its docks and shipyards, chemical, salt and engineering as well as the iron and steel industries.

The Tees had long been used by commercial shipping. Yarm was a small-scale inland port until the middle of the nineteenth century, but at 21 miles from the sea, it was not ideally placed and lost trade, first of all to Stockton. In 1808 the Tees Navigation Co. straightened the river below Stockton and the latter town began to handle a lot of coal brought to it by rail. This arrangement was not ideal because the Tees was too shallow to handle vessels of the requisite size and so the unloading of the coal was moved to a spot just 7 miles from the sea at what was first called Port Darlington and then later, Middlesbrough. The Tees is still busy with shipping.

Henry Bolckow was a German immigrant who arrived in England, virtually penniless, at the age of twenty-one and who formed a fruitful business partnership with John Vaughan, who was from Wales. Their activities diversified to include coal mines, quarries, gasworks, factories and brickfields. Their enterprise was held up for public admiration by none other than Prime Minister William Gladstone. He described the town as 'the youngest child of England's enterprise but, if an infant, an infant Hercules'. The two men are remembered in statues, Vaughan at Victoria Square and Bolckow at Albert Park. Bolckow became Middlesbrough's first Mayor and the town's first MP. With Isaac Lowthian Bell, who leased iron deposits at Normanby in 1853, they stood out as not being Quakers, unlike almost all the other local entrepreneurs.

At one time, Middlesbrough could almost have claimed to be iron-founder to the world. The company that succeeded Bolckow and Vaughan was Dorman Long, and it was their proud boast that they provided the fabric for the Sydney Harbour Bridge. In fact, bridges were something of a local speciality and two fine products of the town's bridge-building industry can still be seen. One is the Transporter Bridge, crossing the Tees to Port Clarence on the County Durham side. At 850ft long and with its uppermost parts at 225ft above the river, it opened in 1911 and was built by the Cleveland Bridge & Engineering Company. The bridge has the big advantage that there is no static deck to provide an obstruction to shipping on the river. The suspended travelling car takes just over two minutes to complete its journey. Originally designed to hold 860 passengers, it is now restricted to 600 passengers and nine cars. At one time pedestrians with a head for heights were allowed to climb 209 steps to cross the river by the gangway joining the bridge's pylon structures. This gangway is 165ft above the Tees at high-water level and gave a view to die for. Unfortunately that is precisely what some people intended and, having sampled the view, they committed suicide by throwing themselves off. Access is no longer allowed. Just to the west of the town is the first vertical-lift bridge installed in England and it has always been the largest of its kind. It is a splendidly ponderous example of heavy mechanical engineering, containing over 6,000 tons of steel. The lifting span is 270ft long and 66ft wide and it weighs about 2,500 tons.

Middlesbrough is a workaday place, the grid-pattern of its streets being evidence of its planned nature and rapid growth in the Victorian period. Tourists do not flock to the town but it has a few fine public buildings including a surprisingly grand, maybe even pretentious, town hall. There is an attractive Custom House in North Street, dating from 1840 and the railway station in an eclectic Gothic is worth a glance, especially since it has been renovated. A museum dedicated to Captain Cook is at Marton, 3 miles to the south. A granite vase in Stewart Park marks the site of the simple cottage in which he was born. In Middlesbrough's Central Gardens is a memorial to Cook which is called The Bottle of Notes. It was unveiled in 1993 and, as with much modern sculpture, it has excited controversy in some observers, total bafflement in others and derision in many. Great Ayton has the Captain Cook Schoolroom Museum.

Middlesbrough suffered appalling environmental pollution because of its position at the centre of this concentration of industries. For this reason its inhabitants were sometimes referred to as 'Smoggles'. The town numbers among its immortals Brian Clough (1935-2004), the football manager, and Chris Rea, the pop music balladeer, (b. 1951).

A distant view of the Transporter Bridge across the River Tees.

Middlesbrough Bridge. This was the first vertical lift-bridge in England.

Redcar

Redcar's development as a seaside resort began in the 1850s and 1860s when a sea wall and promenade were constructed. The next step for any aspiring seaside resort was to consider erecting a pier. The Redcar Pier Company was formed in 1866. Redcar is just on the fringe of what is still one of the UK's heaviest concentrations of industry around Teesside, but it has continued to attract trippers because of its good sands and leisure park.

Redcar benefits from an excellent sandy beach.

It was on the sands at Redcar that Samuel Plimsoll (1824-98), the MP for Derby, was strolling when he got the idea for what became known as the Plimsoll Line. This was a system for marking the hulls of merchant ships with lines, indicating safety margins for loading purposes. He was indignant about the common practice of sending old and unseaworthy ships to sea vastly overloaded and over-insured. The owners sent these 'coffin ships', as they were called, to sea hoping that they would sink and that they would then be able to collect the insurance money. It mattered little to them that the seamen were likely to drown. Plimsoll's efforts met with considerable opposition from the ship-owners who declared that they would be bankrupted if such an idea ever became law, but it was passed by Parliament in 1876.

Redcar has a Museum of Shipping and Fishing which contains the oldest lifeboat in Britain, the *Zetland*, which was built in 1800. It saved 500 lives before it was taken out of service after seventy-eight years. It has an unusual design which allows it to be rowed in either direction. The museum can be found on the promenade.

In the local cemetery lie two German airmen who died during the First World War when their Zeppelin, cruising quietly over the coast, burst into flames and crashed to the ground.

The people or Redcar were sometimes referred to as 'Sandrakers' because of their characteristic of rooting around on the beach gleaning coal, a free supply for the domestic hearth.

Inland from Redcar is the village of Kirkleatham. Dominating the church is the Turner Mausoleum. This peculiar building was erected in 1740 to the memory of Marwood William

These charming model penguins can be seen on the front at Redcar. In the distance is the doomed Redcar steelworks. Britain's manufacturing capacity has gone into free fall in an economy now based on the service and financial sectors.

Turner who died in 1739 while engaged on the Grand Tour. Close by are other examples of building eccentricity, including miniature fortresses and a Gothic gatehouse.

At the time of writing (September 2009), the future of the huge Redcar steelworks hangs in the balance.

Marske-by-the-Sea

Captain Cook's father died and was buried at Marske in 1779. Fortunately, he passed away spared the knowledge that his son had died six weeks earlier. Cook Senior was illiterate until old age when it is said that he learned to read so that he could enjoy his son's accounts of his voyages.

A collector of folklore recorded a curious story in 1898. In much earlier times, the old church had fallen into such disrepair that it was decided that it should be pulled down and rebuilt on a new site, using as much of the stone of the old church as could be salvaged. Most of the local people were uneasy about this decision but there was little they could do to prevent the action going ahead. At the end of the first day, part of the building had been knocked down and the stone carted off to the new site. The men were amazed when, returning next morning, they found the church building as complete as it had been before they started knocking it down! The authorities were informed and told them to get to work knocking the building down again. They left the building half-demolished in the evening, yet the next morning it was once more complete. This happened again and so it was decided to keep an overnight watch. Those who kept watch saw nothing and indignantly denied falling asleep, but in the morning there, of course, was the church whole once more. It was then decided to restore the building after all, much to the delight of most of the local people. They knew what had happened: a hobman had felt outraged about the plan to demolish and remove the church and decided to help them out by bringing the stone back and rebuilding the church. Hobs, or supernatural creatures with similar names, are familiar in English folklore. When so inclined, they can use their powers to help mere humans. However, they can be quite diabolical when the mood takes them. Fortunately, this was a benevolent one.

The attraction of Marske lies in its glorious sands, sand dunes and in bracing walks along the beach.

Saltburn

Saltburn is the creation of the enormously rich Quaker businessman Henry Pease, one of a dynasty who exercised great influence on Teesside in the nineteenth century. His involvement with the Stockton & Darlington Railway led him to advocate an extension eastwards to the Skelton area to open up ironstone mining. Always on the lookout for new commercial ventures, he saw an additional benefit in building a short branch to Saltburn. He was a leading light in the Saltburn Improvement Company, which developed what was no more than a seaside hamlet with a very fine, almost dramatic site into what was intended to be a smart seaside watering place and a comfortable residential town. The railway arrived in 1861 and it was Pease who built the imposing Zetland Hotel with its own railway platform, so that the rich and fashionable passengers could step

Saltburn was just the kind of place, given its somewhat soporific atmosphere, to provide an ideal location for those needing rest or convalescence. This building housed the convalescent facilities for the Working Men's Club and Institute Union.

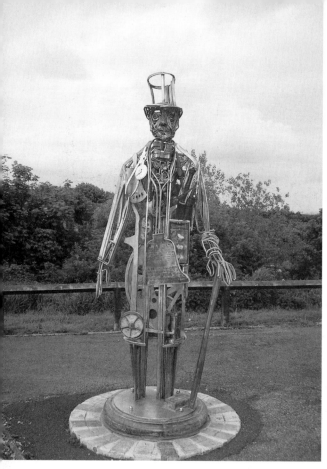

The statue of Henry Pease, Saltburn. The Pease family accrued enormous wealth and set an indelible stamp on the lower reaches of the River Tees with their many economic and industrial ventures.

Saltburn has acre upon acre of gorgeous golden sand.

The spartan facilities of the present Saltburn station contrast with the style of the old station buildings which have been taken over for alternative use.

straight off the train into the hotel while remaining under cover. The enormous, rather gloomy, building is now flats, but in its time it was considered one of the finest hotels in the world. Streets of light-coloured firebrick houses on a grid pattern followed, many of them named after precious stones. They include Emerald, Pearl, Diamond and Coral Streets. Pease originally envisaged a considerably larger planned town of streets of white brick houses, until someone politely reminded him that white bricks were frequently used to line men's urinals. Later, red Accrington bricks were used. In 1884 the Cliff Lift was built to link Marine Parade and the Lower Promenade. This hydraulically operated tramway, which is still in operation to this day, is thought possibly to be the oldest in the world.

Before these improvements, Saltburn had been a tiny fishing hamlet located where a small beck gushed into the sea. There are delightful wooded gardens laid out by the side of this beck. However, the grandiose intentions for Saltburn never came to complete fruition. The Improvement Company insisted on very high standards for the early buildings of the planned town, but in 1875 a depression hit the Teesside industries. This meant less money in the local economy and many of the private developers involved in Saltburn decided that it cost too much to meet the company's exacting requirements. The result is that many of the later buildings are simply jerry-built by comparison. What can be seen now is a distinctly faded resort and

This somewhat gloomy pile is the former Zetland Hotel at Saltburn. Although long disused as a hotel, it gives some ideas of the aspirations that were held out for the development of Saltburn as a prestigious seaside resort for a discerning clientele.

residential town which, however, benefits enormously from its spectacular site, superb sands and attractive woody defiles. The remains of a Roman signal station stands on the prominent Hunt Cliff, over a mile to the east of the town.

Coatham, Redcar, Marske and Saltburn had a strong tradition of smuggling. They were tiny settlements that enjoyed extensive, gently sloping beaches and were largely cut off from inland influences by the Cleveland Hills, through which the roads were notoriously poor, even by seventeenth- and eighteenth-century standards.

The first recorded seizure of contraband at Marske was in 1721, when a local man had the misfortune to get caught red-handed with five half-ankers of brandy in his coble on the beach. Shortly afterwards, preventive men apprehended a smuggling run at Saltburn and seized some unusual commodities, including liquorice and pepper. In 1735 riding officers unearthed substantial quantities of brandy, gin, tea and cambric under a clamp of potatoes, some little distance inland. These were thought to have been landed at Saltburn or Marske.

A common ploy of smugglers was to sink small tubs full of spirits just off the shore. They were attached to a line marked by a buoy and could be recovered when the smugglers thought that the coast was clear. The preventive men would row around checking any buoys. The work was labour-intensive and not very productive because many of the buoys were

Customs Riders. On occasion the authorities commandeered dragoons to assist the local riding officer in his duties against smuggling. What the dragoons thought of this was unprintable.

'Mortuary' at Saltburn. A curious little building close to the well-known Ship Inn.

decoys deliberately placed to occupy the preventive men while the smugglers were engaged in skulduggery somewhere nearby but out of sight. There are surviving records left by the preventive men full of frustration at having been led on a wild goose chase by smugglers in this area.

The doyen of smugglers on this piece of coast was John Andrew. What is known of him is largely hearsay because he appears in no official documentation (something that speaks volumes for his skills as a smuggler). He is first heard of in the area in 1778 as landlord of the Ship Inn at Saltburn, which still trades today and with its position close to the sea remains redolent of the days of smuggling. Andrew's business operations, legal and otherwise, evidently prospered because he built himself a big house up on the cliff-top at Saltburn and used its cellars as a store and distribution centre for contraband. He was part-owner of a vessel built specifically for the smuggling trade. In 1804 he secured a post as an officer in the local militia – which is interesting, given that these part-time soldiers were sometimes called upon to lend a hand to the preventive men. His upwardly mobile path was confirmed when he became Master of Fox Hounds to the Cleveland Hunt. This was despite the fact that everyone knew he got most of his money from smuggling. A must for anyone interested in the free trade is the Saltburn Smugglers Heritage Centre next to the Ship Inn.

Inland are the Cleveland Hills. The most notable of these hills is the delightfully-named and conically-shaped Roseberry Topping. A local weather expression is:

> When Roseberry Topping wears a cap,
> Let Cleveland then beware a clap.

Skinningrove

Skinningrove was built to house the men who worked the iron deposits up the valley of the stream which enters the sea nearby. When the mines closed, steelworks took their place and streams running down to the beaches are still stained by the rusty colour of iron ore waste. The industrial blight of the past and present manufacturing activity vies with spectacular coastal scenery and fine sands. Close to Skinningrove is the Tom Leonard Mining Museum, which provides a fine insight into the history of local mining.

South of Skinningrove, at Hummersea Scar, the industrial remains are returning to nature. There were alum mines here, exploited between 1600 and 1870. The industry declined after a way was found of making alum from coal shale treated with sulphuric acid. The scars left behind by this activity are still very evident.

The highest of the cliffs at Boulby stand 666ft above the sea, making them the loftiest on the east coast of England. A walk along the cliff-top provides superb views across the sea. Inland a potash mine provides an interesting, if ugly, alternative sight.

The story is told that, many centuries ago, the fishermen of Skinningrove captured a merman. They kept it for several weeks, feeding it on raw fish of which it could not get enough. A contemporary account said that it made a shrieking noise but was 'courteous' to everyone who came to view him, being especially pleased when visitors included toothsome young ladies. He seemed content with his lot but one day, when things were quiet, he made his escape and plunged into the sea although, being courteous to the end, he apparently waved goodbye. This story has more than a hint of the apocryphal about it, as has the tale from nearby Loftus where a large and poisonous wyvern was allegedly killed by Sir John Conyers.

The Alum Industry

Alum is a naturally occurring mineral which could be processed into an agent used extensively for dyeing wood, tanning leather and sizing paper. It was possibly used by the ancient Egyptians and the Romans definitely used it to improve the durability of leather. Vain people in the sixteenth century used it to whiten their faces and cover what they thought of as disfiguring freckles. The modern chemical industry makes widespread use of alum for producing such diverse products as depilatories, astringents and deodorants, and in various modelling compounds, a number of vaccines and in the pickling of preserved foods. At one time, it was introduced as an adulterant into bread to make it whiter. It is even said to have been used as a contraceptive. Alum, in a word, was valuable.

Attempts were made in the sixteenth century to locate alum in Ireland, in Dorset and the Isle of Wight. At best, these efforts were only partially successful. Henry VIII in particular wanted indigenous supplies, rather than having to rely on imports from Catholic countries with which diplomatic relations were frequently strained. It seems that the first successful operation involving alum was at Guisborough, some distance inland from the north Yorkshire coast, in the 1590s. There, the story goes, Sir Thomas Chaloner found a number of geological and other natural phenomena similar to those he had seen at alum workings in Italy. Other similar evidence was found on the coast between Saltburn and Ravenscar. The expertise needed to turn the grey-blue shale into white alum crystals did not exist in England and foreigners had to be paid well to come to Yorkshire, but even then it was many years of painful trial and error before good quality alum could be produced in quantities sufficient to make the effort worthwhile.

The start-up costs required heavy investment which was unlikely to produce a quick return. The Yorkshire operations required the removal of large amounts of overburden before workable shale was reached. The infrastructure necessary for extracting and processing operations was complex and expensive, a variety of raw materials, including coal, having to be brought in from elsewhere, adding greatly to costs while a workforce had to be assembled, trained and housed. This included not just labourers and process workers but craftsmen such as carpenters and coopers. The extraction, processing and transporting of the shale and of the spoil produced were all labour-intensive activities. Preliminary operations seem to have started in the first decade of the seventeenth century.

The overburden, which could be as much as 50ft in depth, was removed and where possible dumped in the sea. The shale was then quarried, broken up and placed in heaps which were then burnt or calcined. This part of the operation could take three months, after which the alum had turned red. It had also become crumbly or friable which was necessary for the later extraction of the soluble salts. The calcined shale was then placed in pits, usually clay-lined, and soused and steeped in water, producing what was known as 'liqour' containing various sulphates, especially aluminium suphate. Now the remaining spent shale was thrown aside and the liquor was put into tanks to settle where such remaining impurities as lime, iron and soil would be deposited as a sediment. The liquor was then run off into lead or copper pans and boiled. An alkaline, such as putrid urine or the ashes of the seaweed kelp, was mixed in and heating took place once more. This solution when cooled began to form crystals and after other treatment this was the product which could be made ready for transportation.

For the purposes of the alum industry, urine was something to be valued and the assistance of the general public was enlisted in order to produce this vital raw material. Containers were placed in the streets of Whitby ready to receive the contents of the town's chamber pots. The urine was then stored briefly, during which time the uric acid and urea were transformed into a vital ingredient in the process of making alum. Try as they might, the citizens of Whitby simply could not produce sufficient urine and large amounts were brought in from elsewhere by sea, especially from London. It seems that the best urine for industrial purposes was produced by poor people, who were unlikely to consume much strong beer. The men who manned the ships conveying urine (sometimes euphemistically called 'chamberlye') had to put up with a great deal of ribbing.

The bringing in of coal supplies and other raw materials by sea was no simple matter on a coast which had many navigational hazards and possessed few natural harbours. For this reason, artificial deep channels had to be made along with piers, breakwaters and wharves. It is likely that the needs of the alum industry contributed to the development of Whitby as a commercial port rather than a base for the fishing industry. It may also have been a factor in the growth of shipbuilding at Whitby.

The development of the alum industry was accompanied by costs, both human and environmental. Large amounts of sulphurous and other harmful gases were produced in what would have been low-paid and highly hazardous employment. We can only guess at the impact on the health of the workers in the industry. The landscape was disfigured by all the paraphernalia associated with the industry, by its effluents, its waste-products and excavations. Spoil was tipped indiscriminately into the sea, into rivers or onto heaps. The industry may well have produced acid rain. Great gashes were made in the land by quarrying activities because about 50 tons of shale had to be dug out and processed in order to gain one ton of alum. Time has softened the environmental impact of this activity but evidence can be seen at places like Ravenscar, Loftus, Sandsend, Boulby and Kettleness.

The eighteenth century marked the high days of the industry and developments in chemistry meant that cheaper alternatives to alum started coming into use. By the 1870s the alum industry in North Yorkshire was defunct.

Staithes

Staithes is a tiny, picturesque fishing village nestled between cliffs at the mouth of a small stream, the Roxby Beck. Its most famous son is Captain Cook, who was born near Redcar but was apprenticed at the age of sixteen in 1744 to the village grocer and haberdasher of Staithes.

He soon got bored and fed up with being verbally and physically chastised by his employer. After eighteen months he had had enough. He was so disaffected that one night he took a shilling from the till, put all his worldly possessions in a spotted handkerchief tied to the end of a stick and legged it off to Whitby. He went to sea, first of all as a ship's servant aboard a Whitby vessel, and quickly made a name for himself as a naturally gifted navigator. He worked on coastal colliers and other small merchant ships before going into the Royal Navy. He acted as master and navigator of a ship employed in charting the coasts of Labrador and Newfoundland. However, he made his real mark when he was placed in command of a tough little collier vessel called *Endeavour* which was commandeered by the Royal Navy. The main purpose of the expedition was to observe the transit of Venus and to search for a continent believed to exist in the south Pacific. On board were Joseph Banks and a number of artists and naturalists who drew or collected a huge variety of interesting new plant and animal specimens. The voyage was considered a great success and shortly afterwards Cook was promoted to post-captain.

In 1772 he set off on another voyage, again accompanied by scientists and naturalists. This time there were two ships, the *Resolution* and the *Adventure*. They looked in on the coast of Antarctica and made many important discoveries in the south Pacific, including Easter Island. His navigational discoveries aroused great interest, as did his insistence that his ships carried supplies of fresh citrus fruits to fight off the possibility of scurvy affecting his crews. In 1776 he set off on a third voyage, this time in *Resolution* and accompanied by *Discovery*, and the mission was to try to find and chart the fabled North-West or North-East Passages. Although this part of the expedition was fruitless, much very useful information was gained. Cook's last voyage ended violently in 1779 when he got into an argument with some natives of Hawaii and was killed. By the time he died he had sailed further around the world than any other man, but he had always remained the understated hero, never seeking the limelight.

This part of the coast has been subjected to attack by the sea and, on just one stormy night, sixteen houses disappeared into the ocean's hungry maw. They included the shop in which Cook had whiled away so many miserable hours. It is said that some bits of the building were recovered and incorporated into what is now 'Cook's Cottage'.

It is hardly surprising that a place like Staithes has offered inspiration to many artists over the years. In the period between about 1880 and 1910 some of those who came to the village most frequently came to be known as the 'Staithes Group'. The most prominent was probably Laura Knight (1877-1970) whose husband, Harold, was also a painter. Curiously enough, the couple were part of another group of artists who based themselves in the far west of Cornwall. The Knights spent much time in Newlyn, which was a fishing village having much in common with Staithes. Work produced by members of the Staithes Group can be viewed in Whitby Museum.

The guidebooks say that Staithes should not be missed but frankly it is best visited out of season. Visitors by car are required to park at the top of the hill so that at least the main part of the village avoids serious traffic congestion. Staithes bears more than a passing resemblance to Cornish fishing villages such as Polperro, or Clovelly in Devon, although the buildings here are of sandstone and roofed with red pantiles.

South from Staithes, the 35 miles to Filey Brigg is often called the 'Dinosaur Coast'. The footprints of dinosaurs have been unearthed in the sandstone cliffs around Whitby, while other

A general view of Staithes village.

measures composed of limestone have been found to contain large and clearly predatory fossilised marine reptiles. Sandy and muddy deposits laid down about 160 million years ago in river deltas provide less threatening fossils around Ravenscar. They include leaves, flowers and ferns.

Between Staithes and Bridlington, about 50 miles away down the coast, there are no fewer than six lifeboat stations. Weather conditions and, unfortunately, human error or sometimes simple stupidity, means that that they are frequently called upon. They have always been manned by unsung heroes who between them have saved thousands of lives.

Port Mulgrave

Port Mulgrave was a very basic harbour remotely tucked away south of Staithes; it has been largely derelict for decades. Some of the huge sandstone blocks used in its construction can still be seen. The port was built by the Palmer Iron Company of Jarrow-on-the-Tyne to ship out ironstone as raw material for iron-making in its blast furnaces. The port was built at the seaward end of a tunnel which led inland for about a mile to ironstone mines at Dalehouse. This tunnel contained a narrow gauge railway and the contents of its wagons were tipped into coasters which then went up the coast to Jarrow. The entrance to the tunnel can still be seen. Some of the terraced accommodation built for the workers in 1854 survives on the cliff-top, although the mine closed in 1916 and with it the Port Mulgrave's *raison d'être*. It is a fascinating, slightly eerie place.

Towards Runswick Bay, Palmers built an ironworks in 1856 but it had a short life because in March 1858 a massive landslip occurred which made the place totally unusable.

A fine example of a milestone at Hinderwell, not far from Staithes.

Runswick Bay

A mile or more south is Runswick Bay, a quaint, tiny and higgledy-piggledy village at the base of lofty cliffs with some small inshore fishing boats. The village has a tradition of attracting artists. The settlement to be seen now is the successor to an earlier one which in 1682 slipped unexpectedly into the sea because of the instability of the boulder clay. The cliffs in this area are rich in fossils and especially those of ammonites, a long-extinct but once extremely numerous genus of marine cephalopod mollusc. Their nearest living relative is probably the nautilus. In 1901, when the men were away fishing, the women of the village took the lifeboat out to sea and carried out a dramatic rescue of the crew of a ship that had capsized.

Staithes and Runswick Bay feature in the records of the preventive service. Both communities were involved in fishing and large amounts of fish were salted to preserve it in the days before refrigeration. Successive governments, in their wisdom, taxed imported salt and there are several records of seizures of contraband salt, especially at Staithes. Another apparently mundane commodity which was more expensive because it had duty levied on it was candles. It comes as no surprise, therefore, to find them featuring on inventories of impounded contraband. The Staithes smugglers had the reputation of being exceptionally violent.

Kettleness stands on the cliff-top and shows evidence of the former presence of the railway line north from Whitby to Loftus, Saltburn and Middlesbrough. This was a difficult railway to operate but it offered travellers spectacular coastal views. A curiosity was unearthed by archaeologists excavating a Roman lookout station in the vicinity. They dug out the bones of a man with a dog at his side, its paws on his shoulders.

Just along the coast from the village is Hob Holes. This is a large cave believed locally to have been inhabited by a hob, a benevolent spirit who assisted the local community by curing people of whooping cough. The cliffs around Kettleness were once haunted by a huge black spectral hound, or so it was said.

Sandsend

This is a quaint, scattered village with lovely walks inland up sylvan glades and along the sides of babbling brooks, including one to the ivied ruins of Mulgrave Castle in the nearby woods. Just to the north are the remains of alum mines worked from 1615 until 1867. To the south, stretching towards Whitby, is nearly 3 miles of superb sands.

The coast road (A174), going northwards out of the village, climbs the precipitous Lythe Bank and passes the Church of St Oswald before it reaches Lythe itself. The churchyard, at around 450ft, provides superb views out to sea and towards Whitby. The church is ancient but was heavily restored around 1910. There are many fragmentary pieces of Saxon and Norman carving including, for devotees of the ilk, a green man. On display in the church are two ophicleides, which are a type of primitive wind instrument. Before the days of organs in churches, musical instruments were used to provide an accompaniment to the choral parts of the service. There are many memorials to the Phipps Family who occupied the eighteenth-century mock-medieval Mulgrave Castle. The ruined predecessor of this castle was probably crenellated in the twelfth century, but it became derelict after the English Civil War when it was a bastion of support for the Royalist cause. There are remains of a rectangular keep and curtain walls.

Mulgrave Castle came to prominence in the 1850s when the Indian aristocrat known as Prince Dhuleep Singh or the 'Black Prince' took up residence. It is very surprising that this young man fawned at the feet of the British, considering the way they treated him. In 1849 they threw him out as ruler of Punjab and forced him to surrender much of his wealth, including the Koh-i-noor diamond, which was not only sacred to the Sikh religion but also absolutely priceless. He allowed himself to be 'anglicised', firstly to give up the outward trappings of his religion and then to be converted to Christianity. Although many of the British ruling class would have considered him to be no more than a tamed savage, he was charming,

Above: *Mulgrave Castle. Strange to think of this neo-Gothic pile acting as the residence of an Indian Sikh Prince.*

Right: *The ruins of the first Mulgrave Castle, which became derelict after the English Civil War.*

handsome and intelligent; most of all he was rich. He decided to live at Mulgrave Castle. Its owner at the time, the Marquis of Normanby, had little time for it, preferring to reside in London and elsewhere. Prince Dhuleep Singh participated in some aspects of local social life, such as hunting, and is remembered for inaugurating a Sunday school New Year party for the children on his estate. He also started the tradition whereby access was allowed to the ruins of the original Mulgrave Castle and to the formal gardens around the newer castle. In 1863 he bought a mansion at Elveden in Suffolk and shortly afterwards he left the district, never to return. Clearly he was regarded as something of an oddity, and long after he left the district he continued to make news. When his wife died in 1887, he created a scandal in polite society by having a relationship with a young and raunchy working-class woman from London. In later life he seems to have realised how abominably he was treated by the British over his birthright, and he touted himself around attempting to find sponsors for a rebellion to restore him as ruler of Punjab. He was arrested for treason and all his wealth was sequestered. He died, penniless, in Paris in 1893.

Mulgrave Woods had the reputation of being haunted by a frightful bogle or fairy. She was known as 'Jeanie' but it was regarded as the worst of bad luck to talk to her or call her name. A local farmer, however, decided that he knew better and went into the woods calling 'Jeanie! Jeanie!' This so infuriated the bogle that she appeared and chased the farmer. Just at the moment he was spurring his horse to jump a stream, she cut his horse in two. The farmer had little option but to walk home, sadder and hopefully wiser.

In the eighteenth and nineteenth centuries, innumerable small colliers and alum vessels used the tiny harbour at Sandsend and the evidence of the Whitby preventive service makes it clear that the owners and crews of these vessels were not above adding something to their income by engaging in smuggling. With overstretched resources, it was difficult to monitor the movements of so many small ships. A typical example from the records is dated 1723 and mentions a seizure of smuggled brandy, tea and salt in a local house.

4

WHITBY

Whitby has, without doubt, one of the most attractive and atmospheric positions of any British town, inland or coastal. It is situated on a hilly site sloping down steeply to the harbour and the narrow mouth of the deep valley of the River Esk. It is a town of tremendous character with a working harbour, streets of ancient buildings and yet plenty of modern bustle. With an almost palpable sense of history, Whitby attracts more visitors for its size than any other town in Britain, and some days in the summer can not only see traffic gridlock in the roads leading to and from the town but pedestrian gridlock in the narrow streets most frequented by tourists, these particularly being in the old parts of the town on the east side of the harbour.

To the west of the town lie the North Yorkshire Moors. They are not especially high but they are rough, difficult and ill-frequented, possessing a desolate beauty. They have always constituted a barrier to those wishing to get to and from Whitby and the interior. This fact has given Whitby little option but to look to the sea for most of its wherewithal. The visitor is immediately struck by the fact that Whitby is a maritime town. Yet Whitby had been able to draw on its hinterland for necessities such as timber and stone and various foodstuffs. In turn, the people of the small settlements inland have looked to Whitby as their market town and regional centre.

Early Days

It is likely that human settlement started in the Whitby area in the Neolithic or New Stone Age which, for convenience, can be taken as around 4,000-2,500 BC. Many artefacts in Whitby Museum dating from this period have been found locally and there have also been many from later Roman times. When the Romans left, around AD 410, the natives of the Whitby area, themselves the descendents of immigrants who, in many cases, had intermarried with the Romans, faced competition from more invaders and settlers from Europe including Angles, Saxons and Jutes.

The settlement at the mouth of the Esk came to be known as 'Streoneshalh' or, the even more unpronounceable, 'Streaneaeshalch'. It probably developed into an important Anglo-Saxon town. It is likely that in the seventh century, the local people were converted to Christianity at the time of Edwin (r. 616-32) who was the first King of Northumbria. 'Conversion' is perhaps the wrong word. The odds are that they were told to be Christians. Hilda, a distant niece of Edwin's, came to Streoneshalh to found a monastery in 657. A few years later in 664 the great and good of the time came to the Synod of Whitby to debate whether the English Church should follow Celtic or Roman practice. The decision went the Roman way. The existence of a substantial monastery would have boosted the local economy by bringing visitors in, but it would also have been a significant employer of people engaged in the prosaic jobs of serving and servicing the needs of the religious community on the cliff-top, despite the various ups and downs that the abbey experienced over the centuries.

These were turbulent times and dynasties of kings fought over the various provinces of England. There was a marked tendency for raiders to arrive from across the North Sea, do a spot of plundering and sail home with their booty, only to return at a later stage having decided that the country had resources that made it a worthwhile place in which to settle down. They gave up marauding for a more settled, agricultural way of life and over a generation or two they tended to go native. They then found that new raiders arrived eager in turn to plunder them. Many of the people of the area were of Norwegian extraction but the locality was part of the Danelaw, and local place names suggest that there were inhabitants of Danish origins as well. The name 'Whitby' seems to have come into general use, thankfully supplanting Streoneshalh. The abbey was destroyed in 867 by heathen raiders from Denmark.

In 1066 Duke William of Normandy invaded and defeated the English King Harold. William was a ruthless man of very considerable energy and ability, who set out to impose the Norman presence on a largely hostile indigenous population who did not take his presence lying down. In what is called 'The Harrying of the North', he brutally suppressed a number of uprisings and carried out a scorched-earth policy in the northern parts of the country. So much of the wealth of the area around Whitby was destroyed in the course of this that there was little left to register in Domesday.

The revival of the economic and social fortunes of the area began when the abbey was re-founded around 1078. During the Middle Ages, barons and feudal lords frequently endowed monasteries or other religious establishment as it was seen as a way of atoning for life's sins and buying one's way into God's good books. Whitby Abbey was particularly fortunate to be on the receiving end of this kind of munificence and, with a large income from these and other sources, particularly the ownership of land, the establishment and its abbots became powerful forces in the land. In addition, several saints other than just St Hilda were associated with the abbey and pilgrims came to pay their respects and buy items associated with the saints. This generated additional income.

The people of the settlement down by the river needed a church of their own but there was little space down there and so a parish church, dedicated to St Mary, was built close to the abbey. Building began about 1110, just before the growing importance of the town down the hill was recognised when Henry I granted it certain rights and privileges, including holding markets and fairs. Both of these were important for a town seeking to develop a viable economy of its own. Whitby had the advantage over many landlocked towns as it also generated income from being a port. Whitby, as a base for fishing, did an especially roaring trade in herrings. Ships based at many northern European ports could be seen by the quays but Whitby vessels themselves also traded to these ports. In the fourteenth century, Whitby became involved in the coal trade down the east coast with which it was indelibly associated over the next few centuries. When ships were demanded by the Crown for what we would now call 'defence' purposes, Whitby was usually required to contribute ships and men, this being an acknowledgement of its economic significance.

As one of the very few natural harbours along the north-east coast of England, Whitby was frequently used as a haven during bouts of the ferocious weather which the North Sea can produce. Whitby's prosperity has always been bound up with its closeness to the sea. The success of the port in the late seventeenth and eighteenth centuries shows even today in many of the town's distinctive buildings and in its general atmosphere.

It was in the fourteenth century that the existence of a bridge across the Esk at Whitby is first mentioned. This bridge was rebuilt time and time again over the centuries as the traffic crossing it grew in volume. Indeed, it was not until 1980 that a high-level road bridge was built over the Esk Valley south of the town. Before then, road traffic from the north and west wishing to proceed towards Scarborough had to wend its tortuous way through the town and across the bridge. The present swing bridge in the middle of the town can be opened for small coasters and other craft.

The fortunes of the abbey did not follow those of the town. By the time of its dissolution in 1539, it is likely that the roll-call of its brethren was much reduced from its heyday. Among other things, the Dissolution could be described as an asset-stripping exercise. Henry VIII, with quite breathtaking effrontery, seized the monasteries of England and Wales and by closing them down did much to eliminate one of the major bastions of support for the Catholic Church. This he saw as a force hostile to his concept of monarchy. At the same time he tackled his continuing cash-flow problems by selling off the monasteries' assets at bargain basement prices. Then the asset-stripping literally began, often with the removal of the valuable lead from the roofs of the monastic buildings by entrepreneurs looking to make a fast buck, who had paid the King for the right to do so. Whitby Abbey was no exception. The lead was soon off its roof and parts of the monastic building were carted away for use as first-class building stone. The beautiful painted glass was taken away and, more likely than not, destroyed, but the lead surrounds were probably reclaimed. The building must have started to decay very quickly. In this case, the site on which the abbey stood was bought by the Cholmley family, this astute financial move helping to project them into a dominant position in the locality for many generations. They built a large house close to the abbey precincts and helped themselves to fine stone from the abbey.

Often the bells from monasteries were removed and melted down. There is a story that those from Whitby Abbey were taken down and carried off by sea only for the vessel that was carrying them to sink off Saltwick Nab, just south-east of Whitby. If local legend is anything to go by, they can still be heard ringing from time to time. Such a story is not unique to Whitby and needs to be taken with a good old-fashioned pinch of the proverbial salt.

It is worth mentioning that the existence of street names like Flowergate and Baxtergate in the town should not be taken as indications that Whitby was ever a walled town, as it was not. These names are of Danish origin and the stem 'gate' approximates to 'street'. A 'baxter', for example, was a baker.

Whitby Looks to the Sea

It seems that the closure of the abbey either coincided with or contributed to a period of the doldrums for the town's economic fortunes but events took a turn for the better, not least with the development in the sixteenth century of a substantial shipbuilding industry in the town, on both sides of the river upstream from the bridge. There is a record that Andrew Dickson built the *Great Neptune* in 1626 which, with a displacement of 500 tons and armed with forty guns, was the largest English merchant ship at the time. The industry really took off in the late seventeenth and early eighteenth centuries to the extent that Whitby, on a couple of occasions, was identified as the second most important shipbuilding town in England, at least in terms of numbers of ships launched. Major ancillary industries such as ship-repairing, rope-making and sail-making developed at Whitby along with all the other minor business concerns necessary to make sure that ships were ready for and could be kept at sea. These included coopers, chandlers and victuallers, for example.

The well-known shipyard started by Thomas Fishburn built a tough little ship which, although launched as the *Earl of Pembroke*, achieved immortality when renamed as *Endeavour*. This was the vessel in which Captain Cook undertook his famed first voyage. 'Tough' is an appropriate word to describe much of the output of Whitby's shipbuilding industry. The collier brigs were simple, but extremely sturdy, little vessels while the whalers were specially strengthened in order to cope with ice-floes. Very large numbers of small wooden-hulled sailing ships were launched at Whitby and later the yards produced substantial numbers of steam ships with wooden hulls. However, as iron came to be used increasingly in the construction of ships and ships themselves grew larger, Whitby, being somewhat remote from the necessary raw materials and with the Esk being relatively narrow and shallow, was unable to compete with yards on the Tyne and Wear, for example. For all that, its record of shipbuilding is impressive. Between 1800 and 1816, 331 ships were launched there. From 1871 to 1902 just one yard alone launched 116 steamships of up to 6,000 tons.

The port area of Whitby would have been a hive of activity but it is likely that many of the ships registered at Whitby were involved in general carrying work and may have visited their home port infrequently. Whitby ships carried wool, coal, fish, timber, masts and spars for ships, alum and a host of other cargoes, but few as bizarre as the urine, mostly produced by Londoners, that was used by the alum industry. Whitby ships were also hired as transports by the Royal Navy and some even transported convicted felons to Australia to serve out their terms of penal servitude during the late eighteenth and part of the nineteenth centuries. Over the centuries, the mouth of the Esk has been built up with piers and made narrower to increase the tidal scour of the river, but even so it has continued to require constant dredging to allow the larger vessels access. The requirement to dredge has clearly had an impact on the long-term fortunes of the local shipbuilding industry.

There was a price to pay for Whitby's intimate relationship with the sea. Seaborne raiders and invaders have been mentioned, and pirates were a hazard over several centuries. While most pirates were foreign, before the days of the Royal Navy other ports around the British coast might send out ships eager to plunder the commerce of their rivals. In the twelfth century, for example, Scottish raiders came ashore, stole various valuables from the abbey and seized as much of its livestock as could be taken reasonably easily down to the sea. In the fourteenth century, Flemish pirates were particularly troublesome and there was often bother with the French. With the number of prime seamen to be found at any one time in Whitby, it is not surprising that the town also suffered from the attention of the pressgangs.

Large numbers of ships have gone aground along this coast and many have come to grief on the Scaur, which is the rocky foreshore under the East Cliff. Over the centuries there must have been many Whitby men who perished at this spot.

Whitby acquired its first lifeboat in 1802 and many more followed. The early ones were rowed vessels. In turbulent sea conditions it required not only great physical strength from the oarsmen but also superb seamanship even to get them through the narrow gap between the harbour piers, let alone to assist any vessel in distress in the open sea. In 1841 four brave men died when the lifeboat overturned while going to attempt the rescue of two fishing boats. A worse disaster occurred in February 1861 when, during an appalling storm, the lifeboat

managed to rescue the crews of five beleaguered ships and was returning to assist a sixth when, watched by hundreds of horrified spectators, it capsized. There was only one survivor from the thirteen men on board.

On 30 October 1914, Whitby witnessed one of the worst tragedies in its long history of adversity. The *Rohilla* was a hospital ship which ran aground on rocks close to the harbour mouth. Large crowds turned out to watch, horrified that they were impotent to influence the appalling scene unfolding before them. Time and time again the lifeboat went out performing miracles of heroism. Of the 229 people on board *Rohilla*, more than eighty died.

Pier Lane, climbing steeply from the west side of Whitby harbour.

Whitby Abbey and St Mary's Church

On the East Cliff are the jagged remains of Whitby Abbey, providing a landmark for miles, and so conspicuous that they acted as a guide to the German cruisers that dashed across the North Sea in the First World War and shelled a number of towns on this part of the coast. The main purpose of this action was to lure units of the Royal Navy into retaliatory action which it was hoped would bring them into a newly-laid minefield, causing maximum damage to the British for little or no loss on the part of the Germans.

The abbey was a Benedictine establishment of considerable size and importance. The (ritual) east end viewed from across the abbey pond must have been painted hundreds of times and photographed hundreds of thousands of times. It is surely one of the most-easily recognised of Britain's monastic ruins, exposed on its cliff-top to everything the elements can throw at it but somehow the jewel in Whitby's crown. The establishment that arose out of the ruins of St Hilda's original abbey was in the Norman style, although nothing significant of that period survives. What can be seen today is predominantly work put up during a thirteenth- and fourteenth-century rebuilding. It seems that the bulk of the nave, as well as the south aisle and the south transept, collapsed in the 1760s and the central tower certainly came down in 1830. None of the monastic buildings survive, although excavations have found traces of them. What can be seen today is only a fragment of a sizeable and impressive establishment, but the visitor is struck by the high quality of the surviving stonework. Much of this is Aislaby sandstone, excavated about 3 or 4 miles inland. The fame of this stone spread far and wide and large quantities of it were shipped out of Whitby for building purposes elsewhere. The labour involved in moving the stone scarcely bears thinking about. The quarries were above the north bank of the Esk, and the blocks were put onto wagons and somehow manoeuvred down the steep slope to the river where they were loaded into boats and carried downstream to the

Whitby Abbey. The abbey is the leitmotif of Whitby. This is a well-known view, taken looking out to sea.

The ruins of the Benedictine abbey. These ruins may have been knocked about a bit but this was clearly a large and rich establishment.

bottom of the hill on which the abbey stands. It was unloaded once more and placed in more wagons hauled by oxen which somehow managed to heave it up the side of the valley.

The ghost of the saintly Hilda is supposed to appear on occasions, high up on the abbey ruins, wearing a shroud. Constance de Beverley was a nun who broke her vows of chastity and became over-friendly with a local man. (Some say he was a monk.) The sobbing ghost of Constance has also been seen lurking around the abbey precincts, her soul perhaps condemned forever to take spectral form and perambulate restlessly close to the scene of her sins. Also reputedly observed from time to time is a coach drawn by four phantom horses which periodically charges across the cliff-top in the vicinity of the abbey and then plunges off the 300ft-high cliffs. This example of reckless driving is perfectly understandable given that the horses and the coachman are headless.

Close by is Abbey House. This is really the collective name for a conglomeration composed of buildings standing where some of the conventual buildings may have been. As mentioned earlier, the Cholmley family built a house near to the abbey after the Dissolution. This was around the 1580s and it was remodelled in the 1630s. It underwent further work in the Victorian period. Between 1672 and 1682 the Cholmleys built a Banqueting Hall. It must have been a magnificent building because there was nothing understated about the Cholmleys. But, even they could not dictate to Boreas and it was severely damaged in a storm in the middle of the eighteenth century. This seems to have discouraged the family and they eventually evacuated this site and took themselves off to another of their estates. The remains of the Banqueting Hall present a blank-eyed and roofless shell. It is rather spooky and adds another dimension to the immense sense of history and place that exists in this fabled spot.

Third in this trio on the cliff-top is the squat little parish church of St Mary. This is an extremely atmospheric building and the view from it down the steep cliff into the town is unquestionably one of the most memorable in Britain. It is so popular with visitors that it is probably best visited out of season. The glory of St Mary's does not lie in its size or grandeur but in the glorious confusion of its largely un-restored internal fittings and furnishings. The fabric contains work of almost every period from Norman onwards but it is as if each successive generation has added a bit from its own time and taste, with the result that what can be seen now is the most odd and delightful hodgepodge of a church interior imaginable. Even the learned but austere art historian Sir Nikolaus Pevsner said, 'It is one of the churches one is fondest of in the whole of England.'

Among the features that should on no account be missed in St Mary's is a triple-decker pulpit. These were fashionable in the seventeenth and eighteenth centuries when they were often built in conjunction with the fitting-out of the church with high-backed box pews. On these 3-decker pulpits, the lowest position was occupied by the clerk, the middle one by the man appointed to read the scriptures and the highest tier by the preacher. Two ear trumpets can be seen behind the pulpit. They are relics of the deaf wife of a nineteenth-century vicar. A large stove stands in the body of the church, spoiling the view but it is still used. So many pews and galleries have been inserted into this church and bits added on that its medieval origins are not immediately obvious. There is an ornate private pew belonging originally to the Cholmley family, perhaps the town's most prominent family for several centuries. It has odd

St Mary's Church, Whitby. The church is worth climbing to, not only for the view but because inside the lack of systematic restoration makes it seem like a church that time forgot.

corkscrew pillars and, like the family, tends to stand out. There is good stained glass by Kempe of the late nineteenth century. Some of the box pews bear the scars of the graffiti carved by generations of the town's youths, some of whom were probably already apprenticed to the sea. They toiled away during interminable sermons, the box pews providing cover for their surreptitious activities. There are the usual dates and initials and some human figures, but it is the representations of ships which are the most interesting. One example is a crude depiction of the paddle-steamer *Emu* which was a familiar sight around Whitby in the 1870s. The quality of the carving of some of the ships depicted varies from basic and childlike to skilful and, given the circumstances, sometimes remarkably accurate. Does such graffiti qualify as an example of people's art or is it just vandalism? For a historian, it is a source of fascinating evidence with which to interact.

Despite its isolated position on the cliff, St Mary's has continued to be the sole parish church of Whitby, other Anglican establishments in the town being subsidiary chapels-of-ease. It would have been hard to find a location more inconvenient for the townsfolk who wished to worship than that enjoyed by St Mary's, and over the years a source of amusement has been to watch people toiling up the 199 Steps. It is said to be impossible for anyone climbing or descending

The 199 Steps, Whitby. It is worth stopping during the stagger up the 199 steps, not only to get your breath back but to enjoy the view over the roofs to the harbour.

these steps to get the number right. Nowadays, most of those making the arduous ascent are visitors to the delights on the cliff-top.

The churchyard contains a host of headstones and memorials to the men of Whitby who went to sea. Some died of natural causes; all too many were victims of the elements.

Whitby – the Holiday Resort

On the opposite cliff-top, the West Cliff, a statue of Captain Cook looks down loftily on the harbour which was the birthplace of three tough little ships, *Endeavour, Resolution* and *Adventure* which carried him round the globe on his intrepid voyages. Although not born in Whitby, Cook learned his seamanship here. The statue gives some idea of the man – hard-bitten, rugged and absolutely no frills.

This part of the town has little in common with the old port, huddled round the river and the harbour, and was largely green fields until it began to be laid out formally in the middle of the nineteenth century, largely as a speculative venture by the famous, or some would say infamous, railway entrepreneur, George Hudson of York. He controlled the railway to Pickering, Malton and thence York and was looking to boost the traffic and profitability of the line. The West Cliff Estate contains the elegant Royal Terrace, at least part of which was designed by John Dobson, an architect famed for the work he did in the city centre of Newcastle-on-Tyne. The idea was to develop a fashionable seaside watering place at Whitby and here, on the West Cliff, was to be the accommodation for its middle-class clientele. The development was never finished because Hudson was found to have been involved in various financial imbroglios which brought him down. His fall was rapid. The momentum of development ceased after that.

The cliff up to the estate was cut away to provide an easily graded road up from the harbour area. This quickly became known as 'the Khyber Pass', an indication of interest in Britain's imperialist activity in the north-western extremities of India.

Whitby had, indeed still has, a greater diversity of attractions than many other seaside watering places. It has never really set out its stall to be a major seaside resort and has tended to appeal to people who are not looking for the noisy and boisterous amusements available at various other seaside resorts. Even today, the small amount of razzmatazz on offer at Whitby is strictly confined.

The fact that it has traditionally been somewhat difficult to reach has also influenced the town's development as a watering place. One largely forgotten aspect of its history as a place of recreation is that an attempt was made to participate in the vogue for imbibing supposedly therapeutic waters. Local business people opened up three wellheads in the nineteenth century. In these, for a fee, the waters could be sampled and drinking vessels were provided for the purpose. Now Whitby never really took off as a spa, perhaps because dozens of other places, more readily accessible, were also trying it. The only visual reminder of this obscure piece of the town's past is a small brick building with a conical roof at the rear of Broomfield Terrace. The water is chalybeate, or iron-bearing, and said to taste not unlike the water at Tunbridge Wells. In 1910 this water could be bought for two pence a glass.

The Crescent was intended to be the crowning glory of the West Cliff development in Whitby. From this angle it looks quite impressive but the Crescent was never completed.

Church Street, Whitby. In the evening, after the visitors have gone home, you can look at the buildings and savour the atmosphere.

The extraordinary rise of the popularity of day or weekend breaks, or longer holidays, at the seaside in the nineteenth century largely passed Whitby by. The popular resorts depended on catering for mass inundations of working people, many of whose jobs, workplaces, homes and surroundings were so dismal that they scrimped and saved all year just to be able to afford a few days' blow-out by the sea. The desire to indulge in an orgy of hedonistic escapism left little time for the rather more genteel and sometimes even cerebral activities that Whitby was able to provide. Besides that, reaching Whitby by train from any distant place took a long time and was expensive. Most of Whitby's nineteenth-century visitors came by train, but then they had the time and the money to do so. When they got there, they did not want to be surrounded by what they thought of as the unwashed masses.

The difficulty of reaching Whitby, at least before the days of generalised car travel, tended to exclude the more proletarian type of visitor, which is not to say that Whitby has ever really seen itself as 'exclusive'. The town has somehow managed to remain an essentially workaday place.

Whitby and Whaling

Close to Cook's statue on the West Cliff is an arch made from the jawbones of a whale, a reminder of Whitby's history as a whaling port. In fact, it is slightly fraudulent because the whale was caught by a Norwegian ship and the arch was only erected in 1960. In earlier

The whale jawbones, one of Whitby's well-known landmarks.

times several whale jawbones could be seen around the town. Between 1753 and 1833, 2,761 whales were brought back to Whitby and their blubber was boiled on the quayside to make oil. As early as 1825 the streets of Whitby were lit by a gas made from whale oil. Whitby's most famous whaling skipper was Captain Scoresby Senior who, as well as inventing the 'crow's nest' – one of those rather obvious things which seem just to have been waiting for someone to invent it – accounted for a personal total of 533 whales. These days we find that a rather distasteful record. With a government bounty of forty shillings per ton of whale oil, large profits could be made. By the 1840s, the great days of the Greenland whaling industry were well and truly over, simply the result of uncontrolled short-term greed. Whitby's last whaling vessel went out of service in 1827 (although some accounts say 1837).

The younger Scoresby also made a name for himself as a whaling skipper, but went on to greater fame as an explorer, navigator and scientific surveyor who provided fascinating logs of his voyages around the Arctic regions. Despite the fame that had come his way, he later left the sea, took holy orders and became the vicar of Bradford. Many items relating to the Scoresbys can be viewed in Whitby Museum.

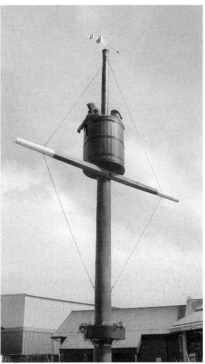

A plaque recording the achievements of William Scoresby, one of Whitby's notable past residents.

Close to Endeavour Wharf at Whitby is this modern sculpture showing Scoresby peering out of his own invention, the crow's nest.

Whitby Jet

The famous Whitby jet is fossilised wood from an extinct tree not dissimilar to the monkey-puzzle tree or 'araucaria'. This wood was subjected to chemical action as it lay in stagnant water and then flattened by enormous pressure over a period of something like 180 million years. It has been valued for ornamental use since the Bronze Age and was greatly treasured by the Romans. In medieval times it was regarded as a potent charm against witchcraft. Jet has the fascinating property of picking up pieces of paper, light fabric or straw after being rubbed on wool or silk: the result of static electricity. Jet is extremely light and can take sufficient polishing to make an effective mirror. Although brownish in an unrefined state, it is unique in the degree of its blackness after it has been expertly polished – hence the expression 'as black as jet'.

Jet is found in several locations in the Northern Hemisphere, but among the most prolific sources have been various locations within 20 or 30 miles of Whitby where, in geological terms, the Jurassic and Upper Liassic rocks meet. It was mined in thin seams in soft shales or sometimes in nodules reached by tunnels or adits. Spoil heaps from this mining activity can be found on the moors to the west of Whitby. It could never be mined in huge quantities, which meant that it was well worth going after as it popularity rose in fashionable circles in the eighteenth century. Pieces of jet are sometimes picked up on the beaches at such places as Runswick Bay and Robin Hood's Bay.

In Victorian times, demand for jet rose to unprecedented levels as the Queen introduced jet jewellery into Court circles as a mark of mourning for Prince Albert. The Victorian fashionable classes decked themselves out in black with ornaments made of jet. This made it a sought-after product and, as so often happens, what starts out as the prerogative of the rich and fashionable, then became very popular – in this case as a souvenir bought by those who came to Whitby and Scarborough by cheap excursion train in the second half of the nineteenth century. Jet could be easily carved and much of the mourning jewellery had the initials 'IMO' meaning 'In memory of'. One advantage it had over potential rivals was its lightness, which meant that even an ostentatiously large piece of jewellery made of jet weighed very little. Jet became a 'semi-precious stone' and enjoyed cult status until cheaper synthetic substitutes appeared on the market in the twentieth century.

Local people who worked jet at the peak of its popularity were convinced that it was a substance rather like amber, in other words, a solidified resin. Be that as it may, it became extremely important in the economy of this part of Yorkshire and at one time an estimated 1,500 men, women and children obtained their living through the jet industry. Actually creating ornaments out of jet was filthy work. After eye-catching amounts of jet were exhibited at the Great Exhibition of 1851, the local industry enjoyed a great boost when the Queen of Bavaria ordered a chain of jet over 6ft long while the Empress of France sent for two jet bracelets.

A small-scale industry also reflecting the geology of the area was that which extracted fossilised ammonites, tidied them up and even gave them small jewels for eyes. These were sold locally, many people who bought them thinking they were petrified snakes.

Literary Associations

It is not surprising that the haunting, unique atmosphere of Whitby means that it has many literary allusions and associations. The earliest of these relate to Caedmon, a humble and illiterate herdsman probably employed at the abbey, who is supposed to have had a vision or experience in which he suddenly and miraculously gained the power to sing and compose poetry. He became a monk at the abbey in around 670. Little of what is known to be his work has survived but he is regarded by some as the first English poet.

Charles Lutwidge Dodgson (1832-98) stayed in Whitby in the summer of 1854 while he was an Oxford undergraduate and before he adopted his *nom de plume* of Lewis Carroll. His first published literary work may well have been small pieces in the *Whitby Gazette*. Although the 'Alice' stories were written many years later, the stretch of sands from Whitby to Sandsend is thought by some to have inspired the poem in *Through the Looking-Glass* where the Walrus and the Carpenter were walking along the beach and weeping profusely because there was so much sand. Shortly after that they dined on large numbers of oysters who they had conned into taking a walk with them on the sands. Dodgson was a deeply complex man. Undoubtedly best known for *Alice's Adventures in Wonderland* and *Through the Looking-Glass*, he was an Oxford Don and lecturer in mathematics. He was also an expert logician. A story that may be apocryphal says that Queen Victoria was so highly delighted on reading *Alice's Adventures in Wonderland* that she wrote a letter to him expressing both her pleasure with the book and a request that he send her another example of his output. A couple of weeks later the bemused monarch took delivery of his *Syllabus of Plain Algebraical Geometry*. He wrote 255 books in all, fiction and abstruse works on mathematics and logic. Other subjects he held forth on included tennis, billiards, letter-writing and medicine. Dodgson is also well-known for his allegedly lustful feelings towards pre-pubescent girls, one of whom, Alice Liddell, is the prototype of Alice. He fell hopelessly in love with a succession of such girls only to fall out of love with them once they began to show that growth in the upper parts of their bodies that boys and men have always found so fascinating. There is no suggestion that his behaviour with the girls ever actually stepped beyond the bounds of propriety.

The Irish author Bram Stoker (1847-1912) knew Whitby well. He first visited the town in 1890 and it is clear he ingested what he saw, hungrily, probably instinctively feeling that he had found the scenario for the denouement of the horror story that was then forming in his mind. In *Dracula*, published in 1897, he provides a description of the place which holds true today:

Whitby, 24 July. This is a lovely place. The little river Esk runs through a deep valley which broadens out as it comes near the harbour. A great viaduct runs across with high piers, through which the view somehow seems further away than it is. The houses of the old town are all red-roofed, and seem piled up one over the other anyhow … Right over the town is the ruin of the Abbey, a noble ruin of immense size. Between it and the town is another church, the Parish one, round which is a big graveyard, all full of tombstones. It descends so steeply over the harbour that part of the bank has fallen away, and some of the graves have been destroyed.

Stoker sets scenes from the novel in the harbour and on the 'Donkey Road' or Church Stairs, the 199 Steps that lead up through the town to the graveyard and Church of St Mary. Whitby seems to have provided him with just the right mix of an atmospheric setting, creating a unity from the contrast between the beautiful countryside inland and the cruel coastline thereabouts. While Stoker was staying in Whitby, he either observed the wreck or saw pictures of a Russian schooner, *Dmitry*, which had run aground at Collier Hope in the outer harbour and just under the cliff on which the church and abbey stand. Only a huge hound, or perhaps a wolf, survived the wreck and it swam ashore before loping off not to be seen again. *Dracula* is the epitome of the Gothic horror story, complete with eerie Transylvanian castles and vampirism. Lucy, one of the heroines of the story, is unfortunately staying in the town at the same time that the Russian schooner *Demeter* runs ashore in a violent storm, manned only by the corpse of the captain, lashed, rather melodramatically, to the wheel and with several boxes of Transylvanian earth, containing the undead Count Dracula. The latter, in the form of a wolf, then manages to disembark and runs through the town in search blood. The story is either a rattling good read or some of the daftest nonsense ever to find itself between the pages of a book. The problem is that some people who have read it regard it not as a work of fiction but as a record of events that actually happened. Those who want to gorge themselves on the theme can visit the 'Dracula Experience' by the harbour.

Lewis Carroll and Bram Stoker have long had their place in the history of English literature, but another person who seems in the last two or three decades to have risen up the league table of Victorian novelists and who had associations with Whitby is Mrs Elizabeth Gaskell. She is known to have stayed at No. 1 Abbey Terrace in 1859 and this may have provided the inspiration for that part of *Sylvia's Lovers* set in Whitby but which she calls 'Monkshaven'. In it she mentions the whaling industry, the press gang and the impact of wars on the town. Mrs Gaskell displays all her customary perceptiveness and eye for detail. James Russell Lowell was an American poet and journalist who had a love affair with Whitby in the 1880s and 1890s. He wrote about his abiding

affection for the place, describing it as somewhat primitive but also, '…'tis a wonderfully picturesque place, with the bleaching bones of its Abbey standing aloof on the bluff, and dominating the country for leagues'.

Perhaps a lesser literary figure, but one who is treasured hereabouts, was Leo Walmsley, who spent his childhood years living at Robin Hood's Bay. In his novels, which dealt with events on this part of the north Yorkshire coast, Whitby features thinly disguised as 'Burnharbour'.

A plaque commemorating Phil May, one of the best-known cartoonists of his day. Most of his work consists of gentle leg-pulls on the foibles of Victorian urban working-class life.

Many people who have visited Whitby, and seen it without the teeming crowds of the holiday period, have to admit that the place gets under the skin and is actually addictive. Among visitors who tarried awhile in the nineteenth century were literary figures of the stature of Tennyson, Dickens and George Eliot, the painter Burne-Jones and the cartoonist George du Maurier. Phil May, a popular and prolific cartoonist, was another fascinated by Whitby's charms. All, understandably, seem to have been charmed by the place and most of them stayed in the West Cliff part of the town.

William Bateson (1861-1926), a biologist who founded the science of genetics, was born at Whitby, as was Storm Jameson (1897-1986), the novelist.

Foggy Weather. A typical
example of Phil May's work.

FOGGY WEATHER.

"Has Mr. Smith been here?"   "Yes; he was here about an Hour ago."
"Was I with him?"

Frank Sutcliffe

Whitby and Frank Sutcliffe are almost synonymous. Although he started out primarily as a studio portrait photographer (work which he found immensely tedious), it is his superbly composed work recording the everyday people of the town going about their everyday business, and his enormously atmospheric pictures of the old parts of the town, the harbour and its ships, that have ensured that his name lives on. A great respect and affection for what he was photographing is evident in his work. Perhaps he sensed a world and a way of life that was changing so rapidly that a record needed to be made quickly, before it disappeared. His work, however, is far more than a mere record because he raised camera work to the level of aesthetics. In the age of digital cameras, it is humbling to think of all the cumbersome equipment that Sutcliffe had to carry with him on his expeditions, some of which took him into the hilly countryside inland from Whitby.

Sutcliffe was born in Leeds in 1853 of middle-class parents and as a child spent many family holidays in the town. He was eighteen when the family moved to Whitby but his father died shortly afterwards. His father was an artist and it would not be unfair to say that Sutcliffe Junior brought an artist's eye to the composing of his handiwork. He seems to have been influenced by Turner, John Sell Cotman of the 'Norwich School' and various Dutch painters. His early professional photographic work was mostly carried out elsewhere, but he seems to have been unhappy away from the north of England and he established a business in Whitby in 1876. He retired in 1923 but went on to give much back to the town when he took over as curator of the museum and, among other achievements, supervised the successful move to the new premises in Pannett Park. Sutcliffe died in 1941.

Examples of his work can be viewed and copies bought at the Sutcliffe Gallery at No. 1 Flowergate. The appreciation of his work today is in stark contrast with the comparative indifference with which it was treated during his lifetime.

Fishing

Even today Whitby is a fishing port with a substantial fleet of coastal vessels. The most characteristic are the cobles, the design of which goes back almost unchanged to the Middle Ages and possibly before. They measure anything between 17 and 40ft and are recognisable by their sharp bow, low, steeply-angled transom and flat bottom with bilge keels. This design enables them to be hauled stern first onto a sandy beach if deeper water is not available.

The Whitby fishermen's year still tends to revolve around the various seasonal catches. For example, salmon and trout between March and August, cod less so now but throughout the year, and lobster and crabs also throughout the year. At certain times of the year mass shoals of sprats appear close inshore. This attracts mackerel and in turn larger fish wait a distance away to pick off unsuspecting mackerel which have just eaten their fill of sprats. Whitby was one of the ports involved in the annual migration of the herring down the east coast, but herring have been decimated over the last fifty years. Local women used to gather shellfish on the rocks near the town and these were mostly used as bait. Cod and ling were caught using lines containing

A collection of fishing paraphernalia stands on the quayside at Whitby.

as many as 200 hooks baited with mussels by preference or limpets, known in these parts as 'flithers'. The fish market can still be a place of hustle and bustle early in the mornings. Fresh fish can be bought and Whitby is deservedly famous for its fish and chips.

A reminder of the herring fishing is the kippering of herring using wood-smoke. The first kippering business seems to have been set up in 1833 and the tradition is maintained by Fortunes in Henrietta Street, although the herrings are now brought in from elsewhere. The fish are split then gutted, washed, dipped briefly in brine and placed on sharp hooks on a series of battens running up to the roof of the smoke house. When the space is full-up, oak chips and sawdust are ignited and left to smoulder on the floor below. All air-holes are blocked and the fish are suffused in the thick smoke for twelve hours. The whole interior of the kipper house is thick with a black tarry deposit from the fish-oil and wood-tar. Unfortunately, kippers are rarely consumed for breakfast these days.

A Bit of Smuggling

At the end of the eighteenth century, Whitby was probably the sixth most significant port in Britain. Alongside legitimate trading activities, smuggling generated a lot of money for the local economy. Anything made expensive because of import or export duties was likely to attract the attention of the free trade. So it was that, in 1722, the master of a Whitby coble found

An old tiled advertisement on the shop opposite Whitby railway station.

himself having to explain how he came to be in possession of four stones of prunes. He had met a Dutch vessel in the bay and bought the consignment of prunes knowing that there was a ready market for them, given that they had become extremely expensive when duty had been levied on them. Romantic images of smuggling rarely extend to contraband goods like prunes.

It would be very easy to envisage several of Whitby's many pubs having acted as a rendezvous for smugglers, or as a place where contraband goods were stored. It is almost certain that several of them featured in both roles. One that certainly looks the part is the former Ship Launch Inn, now the 'Old Smuggler' café in Baxtergate. A curiosity adorning the frontage of this venerable building is a piece of carving in wood which is said to have been the figurehead from a smuggling vessel salvaged after the preventive service had seized and dismantled it.

Whitby was an obvious location for smuggling activity, being something of a haven for beleaguered shipping on a difficult coast and a busy port which made it difficult to check on all the comings and goings. It was remote from substantial markets where the contraband goods could be sold but, while the routes inland to places like Pickering, Malton and York were not easy to traverse, they were also ill-frequented and carriers developed great expertise in passing through the difficult terrain quickly and easily. In May 1769 a farm wagon was intercepted near Thirsk, about 35 miles from the coast. On board were six half-ankers of gin, two of brandy and

30lbs of tea, all under a load of hay. Much of the contraband that entered Whitby was brought in by legitimate ships and stowed away in hidey-holes on board. For example, in 1770 a collier vessel from South Shields was stopped and beneath its cargo of coal was found an even more lucrative one of gin, tobacco and tea. The ship's captain said he had no idea how it got there. When ships berthed at Whitby, it was alongside the quay and right in the middle of the town which made it simplicity itself for illicit cargoes to be taken on shore inconspicuously in small quantities and then whisked away.

An eighteenth-century preventive officer based at Whitby had the engaging name of Hamlet Woods.

Whitby Museum

As with many other towns in the period 1750 to 1850, Whitby Museum in Pannett Park traces its origins to the foundation of a Literary and Philosophical Society in 1823. In 1827 the society set up a museum in Baxtergate, and since 1931 its collection has been housed in Pannett Park. This museum has a reputation which stretches considerably beyond the town of Whitby. Perhaps its strongest section is that dealing with geology and its fossils, drawing extensively on local finds and taking second place to few other such collections. There are many unusual mementos of Whitby's maritime past and a collection of objects presented to the society by local people who gathered them on their voyages to the four corners of the world. A fine library and a vigorous programme of lectures and exhibitions provide a facility of which local people are rightly extremely proud. As a museum it manages to be both delightfully old-fashioned as well as somehow just what a museum should be. Part of its attraction perhaps lies in its understated eccentricity. As early as 1835, a distinguished visitor to the society's then museum premises described the collection of exhibits as 'antediluvian', which in this particular case can be taken as a compliment. He went into raptures about the fossilised ichthyosaurus on display.

Everyone has their favourite among this cornucopia of curiosities, but for the author the *pièce de résistance* has to be the 'Tempest Prognosticator'. This was invented by a Victorian luminary called Dr Merryweather in 1850. It was among the numerous examples of splendid British ingenuity and inventiveness which graced the displays at the Great Exhibition, staged in the building felicitously nicknamed the 'Crystal Palace' in Hyde Park, London, in 1851. Anyway, the admirable Merryweather brought all his intellectual faculties to bear on the problem of how storms could be predicted. Leeches are very responsive to marked changes in atmospheric pressure, so he decided to make a device utilising this previously little-known property of leeches. Twelve small jars each contained a leech. When an electric storm was on its way, the leeches would respond by crawling up to the top of the jars where their motion activated a bell, thereby announcing to the proud owner that a tempest was imminent. Although apparently foolproof, it was not a cheap gadget and, sadly for Merryweather, it did not sell well. Most people preferred simply to open the back door and ascertain that a storm was indeed on its way by listening to the approaching rumble of thunder. Merryweather once lectured to the Literary and Philosophical Society on the 'Tempest Prognosticator'. The lecture lasted three hours!

Another not-to-be-missed curio is the 'Hand of Glory'. This consists of the preserved hand of an executed felon removed while its owner's body was hanging on a gibbet. Some of the fat from the dead miscreant's body was also removed and a candle was fashioned out of the hand and the fat. This gory object was then used by burglars in the belief that, if it was lit, the effect was to mesmerise anyone who saw it (except the burglar himself of course). The only other museum in Britain to contain a 'Hand of Glory' is at Walsall.

In Grape Lane, close to the river, stands the excellent Captain Cook Memorial Museum in an elegantly decorated town house. This is an absolute must for those wanting insights not only into Cook's own distinguished achievements, but also the development of navigation and exploration in distant and exotic parts of the world in the eighteenth century. On Sandgate stands the Museum of Victorian Whitby, with many items related to smuggling and whaling and its general maritime antecedents.

Festivals

Despite (or perhaps because of) its comparative isolation, Whitby hosts lively festivals that manage to be both commercial and alternative at the same time. In the days of August leading up to the Bank Holiday, Whitby Folk Week sees the streets, pubs and meeting places of the town heaving with all manner of people associated in various ways with keeping alive the common people's muses of the past. Other places in the UK may also have their folk-festivals,

The sign of a former hotel in Church Street, Whitby.

Old White Horse Yard, Whitby. The old parts of Whitby seemingly have dozens of yards which are fascinating to explore.

but nowhere else has two Gothic Weekends a year. Gothic Weekends started in 1994 and were so successful that in 1997 they expanded into a twice-yearly event. In October there is a World Music Festival and a regatta is held annually in August.

In 1159 three local men killed a poor harmless hermit. The Abbot of Whitby was so incensed that he condemned them to death but then commuted the sentence somewhat. To avoid being executed, they and their descendants were required to build a hedge on the foreshore which was capable of holding back the tide. Every year on the day before Ascension Day, local people take part in the ceremony known as the 'Planting of the Penny Hedge' of 'Horngarth'. There are several other versions of this story but the ceremony is real enough. The hedge must be strong enough to withstand the force of three tides.

Arguments Yard, Whitby. Not an invitation to a punch-up but a yard named after a former resident.

Finale

Whitby was once described as 'the petty metropolis of a primitive community shut in by the sea on one side and by wild moorlands on the other, satisfied with its local importance and caring little for anything beyond its limits'. This is a travesty of Whitby's role in history. The town has produced men and ships that have sailed to all parts of the world and by their activity have contributed to the process of developing planet Earth into a single global entity.

The people of Whitby in the twentieth century have every reason to be proud of the town and its history.

5

WHITBY TO SCARBOROUGH

This is a walker's coast where moorland meets the rugged coastline but also where many small beaches are completely inaccessible. Scarborough is one of Britain's premier resorts. The cliffs continue as far as Filey.

Saltwick Bay

Located between the rocky promontories of Saltwick Nab and Black Nab lies Saltwick Bay with its sandy beach. Steps lead down to the sands through cliffs scarred by the remains of alum working. The cliffs at this point contain many fossils.

Up on top of the cliffs stands Whitby High Light and fog signal station. This stands 240ft above sea level and has a range of 22 miles. Its foghorn is nicknamed 'The Hawsker Bull' and can be heard booming at least 10 miles away.

High Hawsker

This attractive village lies a short distance inland. By the side of the road to Robin Hood's Bay a small brick structure with a stone roof encloses an ancient spring. There is an inscription in local dialect recalling the fact that the well was used by the Abbess St Hilda and the nuns of Whitby Abbey. It goes like this:

> Lang centuries aback,
> This wor t'awd Abba well,
> St Hilda, veiled I'black,
> Supped frey it, an' no lack.

Robin Hood's Bay

Like many of the settlements on the north Yorkshire coast, Robin Hood's Bay has a tendency to get pleasantly under the skin. The village and its surroundings have a long and fascinating history – in fact it even has evidence from prehistoric times! Fossil hunters frequently come across the petrified remains of creatures of the Jurassic period. Occasional spectacular finds have included a plesiosaur or two, but more commonplace are ammonites, for example, and belemnites, which were creatures not unlike cuttlefish. The first humans, perhaps just passing through, were probably hunter-gatherers about 6,000 years ago. The first settlers may have arrived around 2000 BC. The burial places of some later generations can be seen on the moors west of the village. Bronze Age artefacts have been found. The Romans had signal stations along the coast in this vicinity. However, events were not kind to the Romans and they left, but in due course many people of Norwegian origin settled in the district, attracted by the fertile boulder clay left behind when the glaciers retreated. Sea-fishing would have been another attraction. They probably lived just a little inland in the hope that by doing so they would avoid the attention of marauding pirates.

It is unlikely that there was a settlement at Robin Hood's Bay when the Domesday survey was made in 1086 but agricultural activity was almost certainly taking place close inland. A small settlement on the precipitous site where Robin Hood's Bay is now located probably developed in the Middle Ages and certainly there was the nucleus of a village by the 1530s, in the parish of nearby Fylingdales. By then it is likely that the community was looking firmly towards the sea. A visitor at the time counted twenty fishing boats. A small harbour developed with commercial shipping and fishing, and over the generations hundreds of its young men have gone on to serve in British mercantile and naval ships. In 1816 Robin Hood's Bay had five large fishing boats and thirty-five cobles, which between them would have provided employment for about 130 regular fishermen. Given this tradition and the expertise that went with it, it was therefore a natural development for Robin Hood's Bay to become a major centre for smuggling. Its natural isolation from major roads was both an advantage and a disadvantage; it was difficult for the revenue authorities to patrol such a remote coast effectively, but equally the poor roads inland and the distance from large urban markets added to the difficulty of selling the contraband. Even today, a maze of little cobbled alleyways, some tunnels and quaint yards evoke a sense that smuggling was once rife in the old part of the village that the locals call 'Bay Town'. Some houses have interconnecting doors through which contraband could be passed and which provided an escape route for smugglers being pursued by the revenue men. It was said that a consignment of contraband could make its clandestine way up the street to the top of the cliff totally by subterranean means, via the myriad underground cellars and passages. In terms of its size, Robin Hood's Bay was more of a centre of smuggling activity than Whitby. 'The Smuggling Experience' is a museum providing information about Bay Town's dark past.

The prevalence of maritime skills in so many of the local men made Robin Hood's Bay vulnerable to the attentions of the press gangs. Contrary to received wisdom, except at times of direst need, the Royal Navy had little truck with pressing landlubbers who didn't know a jib-boom from a hawse-hole, but fishermen and prime merchant seamen were another matter. Although many such local men would have had legal exemptions, a naval captain desperate to man his ship might well have been prepared to take the risk. All the local people hated the pressgangs and when it was known that they were approaching, drums were beaten and any able-bodied men hid. This was comparatively easy given the village's underground hidey-holes.

Visitors often come when the sea is tranquil but it can be a treacherous and dangerous firmament. In January 1881, at the height of one of the worst storms in living memory, the brig *Visitor* ran aground in the bay. A message got through to Whitby but the seas were so mountainous that they could not launch the lifeboat there. Instead, with heroism worthy of Hannibal crossing the Alps, they commandeered eighteen horses and hauled and shoved the lifeboat across the moors through deep snow drifts. They took just over two hours to reach Robin Hood's Bay where it was launched and, at the second attempt, rescued the crew of the brig.

The heyday of fishing at Robin Hood's Bay was in the middle of the nineteenth century when about thirty-five cobles operated out of the village. The traditional fishing boat was the coble, but this began to be replaced by the larger keel boats. However, it was the development of fishing as a highly capitalised industry operating out of places like Hull and Grimsby that made smaller-scale traditional fishing methods uneconomical. Before the railway arrived in the vicinity, fish landed locally would be taken on horseback across the moors to sell at places well inland such as Pickering.

It is unlikely that there is any real connection with Robin Hood if, indeed, he ever existed, but legend has it that he came to the area before the Norman Conquest to help repel Danish raiders. This Robin did, with his usual panache, rolling boulders down on the raiders and finishing others off with concentrated arrow-fire. Such derring-do does not fit in with the normal chronological placing of Robin in the late twelfth and early thirteenth centuries. If the sheer number of places in England that claim connections with the man are anything to go by, he must have been exceptionally busy and he certainly got around. Perhaps Robin is a composite figure of myth and legend. Most people like the idea of the fraudulently dispossessed nobleman who took his vengeance on those who wronged him by robbing them and disbursing the proceeds to the weak and needy. He was a 'hail-fellow-well-met' sort of a chap, a folk-hero.and the kind of rebel that ordinary folk would like to have been but would never have dared. He became the subject of innumerable ballads and folk tales – a kind of spirit of the woodland and of the free-born Englishman. Hardly surprising therefore that many places wanted to lay claim to a connection with him. It may be as simple as that. Lack of concrete evidence has not prevented 'historians' asserting that Robin was a frequent visitor to Bay Town, where he spent much time practising in the archery butts which still bear his name. He is also said to have had a fleet of boats waiting in case he and his 'Merrie Men' needed to get away quickly from England. Some say he had a secret hidey-hole where he stored up treasure. The tenuous connections with the possibly mythological Robin Hood have not prevented Bay Town from having a 'Little John's House' and a 'Sherwood Cottage'.

Some of the village has disappeared as a result of coastal erosion and for this reason a 40ft-high protective wall was built in 1975. So intimate has been the relationship between the village and the sea that, during a storm, the bowsprit of a ship is said to have crashed through the window of one of the inns. This story is probably apocryphal because it also turns up at Staithes where a ship supposedly impaled itself in the front of the Cod & Lobster Inn.

The foreshore, which is not suitable for bathing, is popular with fossil-hunters and, with its rocky 'scaurs', those people (by no means exclusively children) who like messing about in rock pools. There is a small museum of local history. A small, more modern settlement is to be found on the cliff-top close to the car park. As with Staithes, visitors' cars are not allowed down the steep and narrow street leading to the bottom of the cliff.

The old part of Robin Hood's Bay is on such a precipitous site that some of the houses are, of necessity, a curious shape and often have steep, narrow and twisting staircases. This accounts for what are known as 'coffin windows', probably unique to Bay Town. These were placed on a bend in the staircase and were designed to be just large enough so that, when necessary, a coffin could be manoeuvred through the window.

The old Church of St Stephen, about a mile north-west of the village, was built in 1821. It is fascinating because of its unrestored interior with contemporary fittings, including box pews and a three-decker pulpit. The fact that the church has not been modernised is responsible for its large collection of maidens' garlands, a feature which has largely disappeared elsewhere. Although they are now discoloured, these items consist of garlands and gloves which used to be carried by two local girls who preceded a hearse carrying the body of an unmarried girl to the churchyard for burial. This sad but charming practice last occurred in 1859.

Robin Hood's Bay has a number of these 'coffin windows'. The steep slopes which are a feature of the village provide awkward sites for houses. Such a window would be on a staircase and it allowed a coffin to be removed from an upper storey when it could not be manoeuvred down the stairs.

One of the picturesque lanes in Robin Hood's Bay.

Bay Town is the setting for the 'Bramblewick' series of books written by locally-raised author, Leo Walmsley (1892-1966). They were *Three Fevers* (1932), *Foreigners* (1935) and *Sally Lunn* (1937).

At Fylingthorpe, just inland from Robin Hood's Bay and in the grounds of Fyling Old Hall, stands a classic architectural folly. At first sight it could be taken for an Ionic Greek temple, although it seems an unlikely location for such a building. It was built around 1883 to the orders of the marvellously eccentric local squire who kept changing the design, even while it was being built. Squire Barry obviously thought more of his livestock than he did of the tenants of his cottages because this oddball building is actually a pigsty, providing accommodation of palatial quality for the porkers. It is now in the hands of the Landmark Trust and can be rented for holiday accommodation. On OS Landranger Map No. 94 it can be found at SE 936/041.

Ravenscar

Old Peak or South Cheek is the rugged headland marking the southern end of Robin Hood's Bay. A hotel, now called Raven Hall, formerly a large private house built in 1774, has stunning views out to sea. The Romans evidently appreciated the site and the view because they had some kind of signalling station where the hotel stands. When the foundations of the hotel were being excavated, an inscribed stone was found stating that 'Justinianus the Commander, Vindicianus, praefect of soldiers, built the fort'.

The Lias shale in the area contains alum, and workings to extract this then very valuable mineral started around the middle of the seventeenth century. There were two large quarries and a processing works known as the 'Peak Alum Works'. It was in operation for about 250 years. What is left of the works is in the hands of the National Trust.

In the nineteenth century, large amounts of money could be made by speculative builders who developed seaside settlements which became fashionable resorts and watering places. An attempt was made by the Ravenscar Estate Company to start such a resort in 1900 but it fizzled out after just a few houses were built when the developer went bankrupt around 1913. What had seemed like a good idea failed to catch on, probably because the site was too exposed to cold winds howling off the North Sea. Evidence of just how windy it could be the fact that shelters on what was intended to be the promenade were blown down. Traces can be seen of how the streets would have been laid out. A brick works was set up to supply the building blocks for the new town. It was fortunate in being connected to the railway line between Scarborough and Whitby, which enabled its products to be used for other projects elsewhere.

Hayburn Wyke

This is a tiny and isolated settlement off a by-road, with a steep path down a wooded valley to a rocky beach where a small waterfall cascades down the cliff.

6

SCARBOROUGH

Scarborough is a complex, multi-layered town. Its topography is fascinating, with a great headland topped by a castle dividing its twin bays which are very different in character. The North Bay is flatter and more modern while the south is hillier with older and grander architecture and a more sedate feel.

Scarborough's site and situation attracted early human settlement. It has a naturally defensible headland, a relatively sheltered position on the coast, a source of food in the sea and access inland to building materials as well as fertile agricultural land. It is likely that the earliest settlers took up residence on the headland around the early Iron Age (around 2,500 years ago). The Romans were at Scarborough, having a signal station on the headland around AD 370. Traces of this installation can be found in the grounds of the later castle. The Romans had at least five such signal stations between the mouth of the Tees and Filey Brigg but it would have had a small garrison and there is no evidence that they established a domestic settlement on the headland, although there may have been a small dwelling close to where the castle now stands. If possible trouble was spotted approaching by sea, the garrison signalled for assistance, probably using smoke or fiery beacons for the purpose.

Later the Vikings settled here and gave the place its name which means 'stronghold of Skarthi'. Skarthi was probably a Viking of Icelandic origin. This was about 966, but it seems possible that it was sacked and burned by Harald Hardrada who landed nearby on his way to do battle with King Harold of England at Stamford Bridge near York. Hardrada fancied seizing the crown of England after the death without issue of Edward the Confessor. Those who think Hardrada was a bit of a cad will be pleased to know that he was killed in that exceptionally hard-fought battle. The destruction wrought by Hardrada's men probably explains why Domesday contains no mention of Scarborough.

The origins of modern Scarborough lie with a town founded by Henry II, probably in 1163. It would have clustered for shelter close to the castle and St Mary's Church. This settlement gradually extended and its vestigial street pattern can still be traced on a map. In fact, the site was not ideal for the development of a town because of the steep slopes down to the South Bay where buildings appeared around the harbour. Most of the town's buildings were timber-framed at this time.

   The headland, 300ft high, on which Scarborough Castle perches is a superb location for such a piece of military architecture. The first castle was probably built around 1135 and was a typical Norman motte and bailey. It would have consisted of a tall earthwork or motte surmounted by a timber tower and surrounded by a wooden timber fence. It could be described as being a 'disposable castle' – cheap to build and initially only designed as a temporary base for the Normans while they imposed their writ on the hostile people of the area. There were thousands of motte and bailey castles across Britain and most were simply abandoned after they had served their purpose. In the mid-1150s, work started on a permanent stone-built royal castle with a keep or donjon 80ft or more in height. A feature of the castle is the extensive curtain wall. In addition to the castle nearby, the medieval town had defensive ditches and walls and gates of which one, admittedly having been completely rebuilt in 1843, survived until about 1890. This was the Newborough Bar, which was removed because it obstructed road traffic. The defensive capability of Scarborough was tested on a number of occasions. A siege took place in 1312 when Piers Gaveston, who can politely be described as a very close friend of Edward II and less kindly as a swaggering and vapid braggart, was allowed by the King to take refuge in the castle from his enemies, who were many. They besieged the castle and, when the food ran out, Gaveston was forced to eat humble pie and give himself up. He did not have much time to eat the pie because he was summarily executed.

On its cliff-top site, Scarborough Castle dominates the town and is a fine example of military architecture.

Gaveston's ghost is supposed to appear from time to time, walking rather precariously along the top of the castle's ruined walls. The spectre is headless, which of course immediately raises the issue of how those who claim to have seen it can be so sure that it is Gaveston's ghost. Anyway, Gaveston or not, this ghost apparently takes great exception to anyone wandering the castle precincts at times when they are closed to the public and does its best to persuade them that they are not welcome.

Edward was so devastated by Gaveston's death and the events surrounding it that he decided to punish the townsfolk by withdrawing many of the town's economic and other privileges. This assisted the town's decline which became much more marked, especially in the sixteenth century. The castle provided jobs and put money into the local economy but activity there was gradually run down. Scarborough suffered from the growth of rival port Kingston-upon-Hull. The town's hinterland was relatively poor and communications inland were difficult, especially given that there was no navigable river into the interior. Even fishing failed to hold its own. The maligned Richard III liked the town, though. On Sandside overlooking the harbour stands Richard III House, a medieval building extensively modernised in the sixteenth century, where the King is thought to have stayed. Had Richard not died at Bosworth, his love for the town might have raised its status considerably. It should be said that his feelings for the place were not totally altruistic; he envisaged developing it into a naval base from which expeditions could be launched by sea to attack and subjugate the Scots.

The fourteenth and fifteenth centuries saw Scarborough stagnate, at best. As with most of England, the town had been afflicted by the bubonic plague, worst of all in 1348 and 1349 in the outbreak known as 'The Black Death'. This highly contagious scourge spread with terrifying speed, especially in the foetid and overcrowded conditions of the towns of the time. Scarborough was no exception. The Black Death is thought to have killed somewhere between a third and a half of England's population and was a natural disaster having profound economic and social consequences. Lesser visitations of the plague occurred in Scarborough through the next few centuries – the contagion was carried by infected rats on ships and this helps to explain the repeated outbreaks.

In 1318 the town was attacked by the Scots but they wisely decided not to tackle the castle. The Pilgrimage of Grace in 1536 was a protest against Henry VIII's attack on the Catholic Church. On two occasions rebels associated with the movement occupied the town, engaging in random looting and some of the local burgesses retreated to the shelter of the castle. A group of rebels occupied it briefly in 1557 in protest against Queen Mary's Spanish marriage before being rounded up, arrested and marched off to London to be executed.

During the English Civil War, the castle was initially held on behalf of the King but, despite its imposing site and buildings, it could not withstand a sustained siege by Parliamentary forces on 18 February 1645. The siege lasted over a year and although the castle was forced to surrender after scurvy and famine had reduced the ranks of its occupants, such was the fortitude of the garrison that those who were still capable of walking were allowed to leave the castle displaying full military honours. It has to be said that the valour of the garrison was not particularly appreciated by the townsfolk, who had had to suffer all manner of privations let alone put up with daily nuisances such as misdirected flying cannon balls. They had to be restrained from stoning the survivors or at least Sir Hugh Cholmley, the commander. The castle found itself the object of a further siege in 1648. Again it had to surrender. After this, along with numerous other castles used by the Royalists, orders were issued for it to be slighted to prevent further military use. 'Slighted' is a strange word to use, given that the castle was semi-derelict even before the bombardments of the Civil War. The Royalists had been receiving military supplies by sea through Scarborough so it was just as well to put a stop to that by rendering the castle useless for any kind of military purposes. In the event it seems to have been decided that the remains were already too far gone and it was left alone.

Scarborough's coastal position seems to have given the town jitters whenever there was talk of the possibility of invasion. One such time was 1745 when 'Bonnie' Prince Charlie was intent on gathering forces to march on London and seize the throne. The security scare that followed involved the marshalling of men, munitions and artillery, but the work involved was not needed because the rebels, who did not grow significantly in numbers to pose a really serious threat, chose a route along the western side of England and even then petered out at Derby, only to be chased back post-haste into Scotland and subsequently slaughtered at Culloden Moor. An incised stone now in the Rotunda Museum records the ninety-six guns that were assembled to defend the town had the Prince's forces attempted an invasion. Nerves were detected again a few years later during the wars with France. In 1798 a substantial military force was stationed in the town, but there was little for them to do except strut around in their uniforms showing off to the local girls.

Misplaced as these eighteenth-century fears may have been, the town certainly saw and received many shots fired in anger during the First World War. On 16 December 1914, German cruisers dashed across the North Sea and shelled Hartlepool, Whitby and Scarborough. The Grand Hotel, perched in such a dominating position, presented a tempting target and received thirty-six hits. A bombardment took place for half-an-hour and left seventeen local people dead and eighty injured. German shells hit the castle and added to its ruination. This derring-do on the part of the German Navy was extraordinarily damaging to British self-esteem given that it was believed to be God's design that Britannia ruled the waves. Indignant cries rang out, 'Where was the Royal Navy?' Scarborough reverted to form, believing that the shelling was likely to be followed up by a full-scale invasion. Why the Germans should have chosen Scarborough for such a venture is unclear. In the Second World War the usual coastal defences were installed including barbed wire, pill boxes and in this case superannuated naval guns intended to hit back if there was a repetition of the earlier hit-and-run tactics. The guns were not used but the town did have over twenty air raids. The worst of these was on the night of 18 March 1941, when incendiary bombs killed around twenty-five people and damaged over a thousand buildings in the town, many beyond repair.

The Harbour

It would be true to say that Scarborough is not a natural harbour, although the headland provides protection for the South Bay. It is likely that some kind of simple facility existed for shipping before Henry III in 1252 granted Scarborough the right to develop a permanent well-constructed harbour, paid for by tolls on its users. This original pier fell into disrepair and Elizabeth I provided funding for improvements and an extension to this pier. Further improvements took place in the eighteenth century, including the new small outer Island Pier. The Old Pier was further extended and became known as Vincent's Pier, and the entrance to the harbour, now called Pet Hole, was made narrow, the better to protect shipping in the harbour. In 1753 work started on the outer Eastern Pier which provided even better protection. A lighthouse was built on an extension of Vincent's Pier around 1840 and had to be demolished after being shelled by the German destroyers in 1914. A new North Wharf was completed in 1928.

Scarborough began to revive as its prominence as a port increased from the seventeenth century; it became involved in the very important coastal trade conveying coal from Northumberland and Durham pits down to feed the insatiable demand of London. Some Scarborough ships participated in this trade while the harbour was regularly used as a refuge for collier vessels during stormy weather. Scarborough harbour became busy with ships trading to and from Scandinavia and the Baltic. Timber and tar were major imports while there were substantial exports of butter and linen. Perhaps it was natural that shipbuilding developed. Wooden ships were constructed at a number of shipyards, the largest of which was Tindall's, located on Sandside. This was an important yard and it launched 155 ships between 1771 and 1820. Abundant supplies of timber were available close inland but the largest components, such as masts and keels, often had to be imported. The availability of cheap coal led to the development of an industry boiling blubber from whales to make candles and soap and also boiling sea water to produce salt, always a valuable commodity. Pirates entered the harbour on a number of occasions on a hit-and-run basis, destroying shipping, seizing easily movable cargo and pillaging those parts of the town close to the sea. The harbour has remained active ever since and is still busy in the twenty-first century, being a major attraction for visitors.

In the South Bay at Scarborough in November 1861, *Coupland*, a schooner from South Shields, was attempting to reach the harbour mouth in appalling sea conditions but, blown out of control, she went aground on the rocks. Scarborough had a new lifeboat called *Amelia* and it was launched, making an unsuccessful attempt to rescue the crew of the schooner. Two of the lifeboat crew were drowned and *Amelia* had to be abandoned. Three further people who tried to rescue the lifeboat crew were also drowned but the crew of *Coupland* were rescued. Events of this kind have been all-too frequent.

In October 1880, in probably the worst storms in then living memory, a dozen or more ships out at sea were attempting to run for shelter in the harbour. Several sank and only one actually managed to get into the harbour, but was quickly dragged back out by the force of the wind and waves. The lifeboat men laboured heroically, going out time and time again and rescuing the crews from ships wallowing in distress offshore. Amazingly, not one life was lost and lifeboat Coxswain John Owston was given an award for supervising the rescue of twenty-eight men.

St Mary's Church, adjacent to Scarborough Castle, is a fragment of an extremely large cruciform medieval church with a crossing tower and two towers at the western end, these towers probably once being surmounted by small pyramidal spires. St Mary's was founded late in the twelfth century. It was perhaps its exposed position that caused the fabric to decay and some of the building had to be pulled down. Specifically, a violent storm in 1555 blew the lead off the roofs of the western towers and caused them to be demolished. Perhaps the tempest

A general view of the harbour at Scarborough.

was regarded as a godsend because the lead was sold and fetched a good price. What was left of the church was badly damaged during the siege of the castle in 1645. An unusual feature of the interior is a collection of around 200 small memorial plates of brass, most of them eighteenth century, which previously adorned headstones in the churchyard. It had been found that the exposed position of these headstones rendered them liable to erosion and so the brass plates were added. Unfortunately these were frequently removed as souvenirs, or perhaps because the local youths were bored, and so those that were left were taken inside the church for safe keeping. The position of St Mary's ensures a constant flow of visitors toiling up from the Old Town but perhaps less visited is St Martin's in Albion Road. Opening in 1862, this is a shrine for fans of the pre-Raphaelites, containing as it does much work by Dante Gabriel Rossetti, Ford Madox Brown and William Morris. The architect, G.F. Bodley, commissioned Morris's newly-established company to provide many of the furnishings, decorations and stained glass, including work by another pre-Raphaelite, Edward Burne-Jones.

As befitted a medieval town of importance, there were other religious establishments in Scarborough including those of the Franciscans, Dominicans and Carmelites. They were all abolished in the Reformation of the sixteenth century. Much has been written about the spiritual decay of the Church in the preceding period. However, while senior prelates such as bishops, priors and abbots waxed fat, religious bodies were frequently engaged in good works. In Scarborough, the hospital of St Thomas the Martyr cared for paupers while that of St Nicholas looked after lepers. Friars lived as members of orders that mixed with and were close

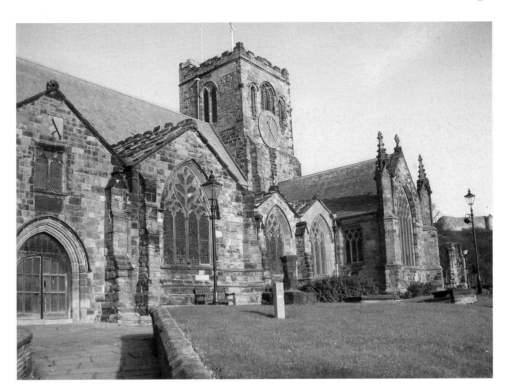

*St Mary's Church, Scarborough.
St Mary's has had to put up with
weather and war and, although
reduced in size, it remains a fine
sight.*

*A comparatively unspoiled street in
the old part of Scarborough.*

to the people. Scarborians must have regretted seeing them disbanded because they had helped the town in many practical ways, such as improving its water supply and paving its streets.

The Spaw

In the 1620s a local woman called Elizabeth (sometimes Thomasin) Farrer or Farrow, discovered springs of unappetising-looking brownish, sour-tasting water bubbling out of rocks onto the beach. She immediately concluded that since it tasted so horrible, it was probably good for anyone who drank it. Clearly an early spin-doctor, she soon announced that this water, if drunk, would cleanse the stomach and the blood and cure asthma, scurvy, jaundice, leprosy, melancholia and various other undesirable conditions. Soon people were thronging to the town keen to take advantage of what were considered to be its health-giving chalybeate or iron-bearing water and also of adjacent saline springs. So Scarborough became a spa before it became a seaside resort. It has always had something of a dual character, acting at one and the same time as a popular working-class resort but having parts of the town which set out to cater for the well-heeled.

Scarborough had an effective early publicist in a Dr Wittie from York. He published a book in 1660 called *Scarborough Spaw or a description of the Nature and Vertues* [sic] *of the Spaw at Scarborough in Yorkshire*, drawing attention to the merits of Scarborough's spa water as a cure for an extraordinary variety of conditions over and above those that Elizabeth Farrow had identified. It should be mentioned that Wittie was a supporter of temperance before that

An engraving of 1733, titled, 'The Antient Town, Castle, Harbour and Spaw of Scarborough'.

concept had become a movement, so he saw the quaffing of Scarborough water as a means of luring the weak away from the temptations of barley and the grape. He suggested that the chalybeate water should be taken both internally and externally. According to him, it dried up what he described as 'superfluous humours', preserved the body from putrefaction and killed all manner of 'worms'. Nightmares, epilepsy, vertigo and apoplexy were just a few of those conditions from which surcease could be gained by taking the waters. In his words, it was a 'most Soveraign remedy against Hypochondriack Mellancholly and Windiness'. Gout, the affliction especially of sedentary, over-indulgent, upper-class men, could be tackled head-on by use of this water and frequent bathing in the sea, or so it was claimed. We unfortunately know all too well about celebrity endorsements in the modern world but Wittie managed to refer to Sir John Anderson who, he claimed, had been cured of scurvy and gout as a result of a regime of Scarborough spa water. This consisted of the daily drinking of eight pints of spa water which, because they allegedly produced eleven pints of urine, meant that each day he managed to rid himself of three pints of liquid containing harmful 'humours'.

It should be remembered that travel was so difficult and expensive at this time that large numbers even of England's richest inhabitants who lived inland had never seen the sea. For such people, the sea would have seemed fascinating, even awesome. A structure was built close to the spa (then often called The Spaw) which took in sea water at high tide and mixed it with water from the spa and visitors, mostly wealthy hypochondriacs, with little to do in life other than to dwell on their real or more often imagined ills, began flocking to Scarborough from the late 1660s. When these visitors arrived in town from May to September, doctors, who were essentially little more than quacks or con-men, would, in return for a handsome fee, prescribe a stay of a month or more with a regime involving the consumption of five to eight pints of spa water daily. That indefatigable female traveller, Celia Fiennes, visited Scarborough in 1697 and described it as 'a spaw well on the beach … covered by the sea at high tide, leaving a brackish saltiness which makes it purge pretty much'. Anything that tackled constipation, one of the banes of upper-class life at the time, was bound to be a hit. No one ever claimed that Scarborough's spa waters or sea water would cure the pox. If they had, the town would have been inundated. When a married couple who had been unsuccessfully attempting to procreate for seven years, learned that the wife had become pregnant after she and her husband had bathed in the sea at Scarborough, this was taken to mean that something in the water encouraged conception. Childless couples could hardly wait to get onto the beach and into the water. However, in a vague and rather sinister way it was hinted that pubescent boys and girls could suffer 'obstructions' if they underwent too much cold-water bathing.

Later books expanded the claims for the local water and argued that it could cure just about everything from consumption to ruptures and from deafness to insanity. With understandable discretion, they suggested that if the reader was the sort of person who suffered with wind, Scarborough sea water was just the right thing. Early visitors, keen to benefit from the efficacious properties of the water, used to leap into the briny in their birthday suits. It was about this time that doctors were strongly advocating the health benefits to be gained from both soaking in and drinking sea water.

A work published in 1734 and entitled *A Journey from London to Scarborough*, gives a lively impression of the early days at this pioneering seaside resort:

> It is the Custom for not only the gentlemen but the ladies also, to bath in the sea. The gentlemen go a little way out to sea in boats which are here called cobbles [*sic*] and jump in naked directly … The Ladies have the Conveniency of gowns and guides. There are two little houses on the shore to retire to for dressing.

Inevitably the presence of nymphs cavorting around in the billows wearing revealingly clinging swimming attire attracted many lecherous voyeurs. Some pretended that their telescopes were trained on the busy harbour. Others were more blatant. It may even have been that, on occasion, young ladies allowed their gaze to stray towards the better endowed of the male swimmers.

The extreme coldness of the North Sea was regarded as efficacious in itself and many visitors came to Scarborough and dipped in the briny in January and February when the water was so cold it made the teeth chatter just to look at it. Sea-bathing over for the morning, there was much else to do at Scarborough. Most people would make a point of drinking the spa waters, in spite of their unpalatable taste. The spa was supervised by a deformed, crippled and generally rather odd-looking man by the name of Dicky Dickinson who was appointed in 1698 and styled himself 'Governor of the Spaw'. Rather unkindly, someone described Dickinson's bearing as that of a person 'about to shite'. Dickinson made a speciality of being exceptionally rude to everyone. This sounds an unwise thing to do considering his largely well-to-do and influential clientele but, strange to say, he was not only tolerated but almost revered. This reversal of the natural order of things perhaps occurred because of the force of his personality and because he didn't pick on anyone in particular but was totally fair-minded – he was equally rude to everyone.

Visitors came in increasing numbers, not necessarily seeking cures but simply because Scarborough was becoming a place to see and be seen. It seemed to be *de rigeur* to scoff some spa water and dunk in the briny but visitors also perambulated the sands, hired horses and rode inland, did a bit of sea-fishing, visited a coffee house, theatre or church or, in the evening, the social highlight being attendance at a ball in what was called the Long Room. Here dancing, flirtation and dalliance with the opposite sex were the big attraction and, for those gentlemen that were so inclined, gaming tables.

Not everyone fell in love with Scarborough at first sight. In 1732, for example, the Duchess of Marlborough visited the town and complained querulously that Scarborough was steep and disagreeable for coaches and sedan chairs, there were no worthwhile walks and far too much sand! The Duchess may have been a naturally peevish character but despite her fulminations Scarborough was on its way up. In 1733 its visitors included two dukes, one marquess, seven earls, three lords and nineteen baronets.

In 1827 access was greatly improved when a bridge was opened across the ravine which separated the spa area from the town. A succession of pump rooms succumbed to landslides or other disasters but a new and larger castellated neo-Gothic pump room was erected on the sea wall in 1839. This was replaced by an improved building in 1858, only for this one to be destroyed by fire in 1876 whereupon the nucleus of the present spa complex was built. It may be called 'The Spa' but ironically no water has been available for quaffing for several generations. An attempt was made in 1995 to provide a new tap surrounded by warnings as to the personal risks involved, but in 1996 the device was vandalised and went out of use.

The spa saloon at Scarborough, 1863.

The neglected spring at the spa. A notice informs the public that the water is not fit for drinking.

By the 1730s, the waters of the 'Spaw' were being bottled and taken by ship or land carrier to London. There doesn't appear to be a record of how it was received there but hope springs eternal and for some people it was simply enough for a label to extol the health-giving properties of its contents for them to believe that it would do them good. It was generally agreed that the Scarborough waters tasted pretty disgusting at the fountainhead and, as they did not travel well, they were even more unpalatable when they had been in bottle for any length of time.

Scarborough flourished because of its early start as a resort offering the health-giving benefits of both sea and mineral waters. Some people came simply because they wanted to bathe and swim. The town is one of several that claim to have been pioneers in the use of bathing machines. By the end of the eighteenth century at least twenty-six of these machines were available for hire. They allowed bathers to dress and undress in privacy, but the downside was that those used by women and children were presided over by female attendants. Care needed to be taken in getting the pronunciation right as they were known as 'Mother Duckers'. They were ruthless in forcing their charges, no matter how rich and privileged, into the freezing waters of the bay, usually insisting that they dipped a minimum of three times. They also browbeat them into providing generous tips. The machines were expensive to hire in the first place.

From the 1730s to the 1780s many of society's so-called elite stayed at Scarborough for the summer season and facilities were laid on for their enjoyment and to try to ensure that they returned. Concerts, dances, bookshops and circulating libraries, coffee houses, billiard rooms and theatres, promenades and public gardens made their appearance to the south of the harbour and Old Town. The more adventurous visitors might hire a coble and enjoy sea-fishing for haddock or mackerel. The spending power of the visitors put money into the local economy but did not necessarily mean generous wages for those who laboured pandering to the visitors' needs. The town had many people living in poverty and squalor but probably in conditions that were considerably better than the heavily polluted manufacturing towns associated with the Industrial Revolution. Not all the visitors were impressed by what was on offer. One disgruntled visitor claimed that Scarborough smelt of fish and excrement.

Towards the end of the eighteenth century and before the coming of the railways, the visitors to Scarborough began increasingly to be of the middle classes. They tended to be less raffish than their aristocratic predecessors and more given to serious and 'improving' recreation such as poking about looking for the curious creatures that lurked in rock pools or using the libraries to research the history and geology of the place.

A Master of Ceremonies was recruited to a job similar to that of the immortal Beau Nash at Bath, this being largely to ensure the seemly and decorous public behaviour of the visitors. One practice which even the most punctilious Masters of Ceremony were unable to eradicate was that of 'skinny dipping'. Locals in seaside places had always enjoyed paddling and swimming and traditionally had always frolicked in the nude. As the supposedly genteel visitors to Scarborough increasingly accepted ground rules of dos and don'ts for how they should behave in public, they came to look on this kind of thing as extremely vulgar. The more they protested, the more the younger local lads took great delight in sauntering about, blatantly flaunting their naked bodies and making provocative gestures at the visitors, whose feelings must have been a

An aquatint of 1813, showing a coach departing from Scarborough. It actually looks more like a private carriage than a stage coach.

Scarborough Lending Library, 1813. Genteel visitors to Scarborough would make a point of visiting the Lending Library.

Bustle on the beach. The skimpy bikini may be one extreme, but surely to wander the sands in this outfit including the bustle is the other extreme.

complicated mixture of revulsion and fascinated compulsion to stare. A man describing himself as the father of a large number of girls aged ten to eighteen, fulminated about this 'crying evil' and with prurient relish described how 'every physical attribute' of the male bathers was 'unblushingly exhibited' and fully visible from houses with a view of the foreshore as well as from the promenade and the beach itself. The answer to the problem was the passing of by-laws making nude bathing illegal. While they were at it, they also demarcated different parts of the beach for the use of male and female bathers respectively. Issues of this nature were by no means unique to Scarborough.

Visitors arrived at Scarborough by sea or road. In some cases they had their own private carriages but many made use of stage coaches. These were more expensive than a voyage by sea but piecemeal improvements to the roads and the coaches themselves made the journeys quicker and somewhat more comfortable. In the 1770s there were four coaches a week to and from London, two daily from Leeds and others serving Hull and Whitby. A more comprehensive network of coaching services had developed by the 1840s but it quickly went into headlong decline, totally unable to compete with the railways.

The Modern Resort

The railway from York arrived at Scarborough in 1845 and had a major impact on the social and economic character of the town. Railways provided a far quicker and cheaper means of transport than anything previous and opened up access to Scarborough for a vastly wider potential range of visitors, including day-trippers. In due course, other lines opened to Whitby, Pickering, Bridlington and Hull. Not everyone greeted the arrival of the railway with joy. Some of the wealthy residents and visitors thought that the relative exclusivity of the town was about to be shattered. They need not have feared an immediate inundation by the hoi polloi. In fact it was several decades before rising real wages and relatively cheaper fares meant that increasing numbers of working-class trippers came to town by train. When they did, a distinction was made between 'visitors' who stayed for a night or two in hotels and guest houses and tended to be better-off, and the 'trippers' and 'excursionists' who came for only a few hours.

Access around the town was expedited over the next few decades by the opening of Valley Bridge in 1865 and such roads as Eastborough, Foreshore Road, Royal Albert Drive and Marine Drive. Four distinct parts of the town could now be discerned. The South Bay was the visitors' quarter with all the facilities of a classy resort but gradually becoming more demotic. The Old Town and harbour area constituted the working centre; Westborough and Newborough the retail district; and opening up rapidly were the myriad of streets around Castle Road and North Marine Road containing many boarding houses and streets of houses for the artisans and working class.

The Grand Hotel perched on its cliff totally dominates its surroundings.

The interior of the Grand Hotel. The hotel may have fallen on relatively hard times but this small glimpse of the interior gives some idea of its grandeur.

A number of prestigious hotels were built in the nineteenth century but none made as much impact as the gargantuan Grand perched on the top of St Nicholas Cliff and itself like an upward extension of the cliff. Its position allowed it to dominate the South Bay and show off to great effect. It contained 365 bedrooms, fifty-two chimneys, twelve floors and four turrets, symbolising the days, weeks, months and seasons of the year. When opened in 1867 it was the largest hotel and the largest brick building in Europe. The ambience which the proprietors thought appropriate is suggested by one excerpt from the rules: 'Ladies will not wear bonnets; gentlemen will wear black frock or dress coats in the dining room.' Even if it is somewhat faded, it still exudes a sense of the huge self-confidence of the Victorian period. It is not beautiful. In reality it is brash and overbearing but it certainly has presence. The architect was Cuthbert Broderick, well-known for his work in Leeds, especially the town hall, and the contract should have been one to die for, except that it was an extremely difficult site on a cliff known to be unstable. Internally, its furnishings, fittings and services represented everything that was at the cutting-edge of best practice at the time and its charges reflected that. In fact it represented the town's last-ditch attempt to maintain itself as a resort catering for the well-heeled. Grand the hotel may have been by name and nature but it never produced much in the way of dividends for the shareholders.

Another notable development was the opening in 1877 of an aquarium larger than any other in the world at that time. This was the work of the Marine Aquarium Company, and while obviously intended to be a profitable venture it was also designed to appeal to the reasonably well-off visitors who enjoyed mental stimulation and self-improvement on their holiday as opposed to merely plonking themselves on a bench and watching the world go by. Admission charges were pitched at a level deliberately intended to exclude the less well-off seekers of mental stimulation. The timing of this venture was apt because there was a fashion for such establishments. This one was decorated with Indian motifs, again very apt because India and things associated with the subcontinent were enjoying a vogue. Prime Minister Disraeli had astutely flattered and rebranded the reclusive and increasingly unpopular Queen Victoria as Empress of India – mother of an empire. This was as a counter to strong stirrings of republicanism. Doing Indian was therefore chic. If an aquarium can be called a white elephant, then this was one and it never paid its way. The only way forward was to broaden its appeal by reducing charges and 'dumbing down'. While it still displayed some marine creatures, it also had a menagerie of land animals and various gimmicks and side-shows, including an 'electric lady' who gave you a shock if you touched her and a woman whose eyes apparently registered the time of day.

As well as having a naturally spectacular site, Scarborough made the most of itself by developing a wealth of public parks and gardens, sports, recreational and other attractions for the visitors. The local authorities were always canny enough to provide amenities that would appeal to the different classes who descended – and indeed still do descend – on the town. The area around Sandside and along Foreshore Road is loud and brash and would not look out of place in Blackpool or Southend, but the advantage of Scarborough is that it is always possible to get away from the noise and hurly-burly. Scarborough carved out a role for itself in the nineteenth century as a health resort and residential retirement town for the middle classes, something of a retail centre and a more 'cheap and cheerful' resort for the working classes, especially from the industrial West Riding of Yorkshire. Before holidays with pay existed, they tended to come on day trips. As far as the local economy was concerned, working-class visitors made up for in numbers what they lacked in spending power as individuals. The town had its industries, especially shipbuilding, a busy port providing many jobs (both land-based and on the ships registered there) a declining workforce engaged in fishing and it had tourism. The moderately wealthy people who settled in Scarborough employed large numbers of domestic servants, at least until the First World War. With the winning of virtually universal holidays with pay, Scarborough, in common with other British seaside resorts, enjoyed its heyday from the 1930s to the 1960s.

One of Scarborough's well-known, if somewhat curious, landmarks is the Rotunda Museum which was opened in 1829 under the auspices of the local Philosophical Society. The most conspicuous feature is the rotunda itself which, lit from above, provided daylight and was considered to be the most effective way of showing off to best advantage the geological collection of the well-known palaeontologist William Smith. Money ran out and the projected wings were not built until 1861. The Rotunda Museum was described by an avid traveller to, and critic of, England's spas, as 'a most delightful source of amusement and intellectual gratification'. It is near the junction of Valley and Foreshore Roads, and in it hangs what is known as the Pancake Bell. It used to hang in St Thomas's Hospital which looked after paupers but has long since been demolished. On Shrove Tuesday or 'Pancake Day' it is still rung at noon to tell local women that it is time to make their pancakes. In an earlier, more religious society, making pancakes was a tasty way of finishing off any left-over eggs before the austerity of Lent. It is still the signal for local people to go onto the beach nearby and skip for all they are worth, possibly as a relic from the days when skipping was thought to encourage the fertility of the soil. In this case it perhaps encourages a good harvest of fish.

The North Bay, which did not really start to be exploited until the later years of the nineteenth century, was where Scarborough's not particularly successful pleasure pier was built (*see* chapter 14). Building development to the north of Scarborough took place vigorously in the period between the First and Second World Wars. Great improvements were made to Peasholm Park and a popular miniature railway was opened running about a mile from Peasholm to Scalby Mills. The famous open-air theatre was built. The first of the twice-weekly mock naval battles was fought on the lake at Peasholm Park in 1927.

In the 1950s as many as 3 million visitors a year still flocked to Scarborough, but from the 1970s the nature of the town's holiday business began to change. The day of the cheap

The curiously shaped Rotunda Museum at Scarborough.

foreign holiday had arrived and there was an increasing range of other attractions both at home and abroad to compete for the spare cash of those looking for recreation and entertainment. The large and luxurious hotels started to close. Those people who continued to come wanted central heating and en-suite facilities. With their income down, most hotels could not afford expensive modernisation. Many of them were converted to self-catering holiday flats or apartments for elderly residents. The Grand Hotel was bought by Butlins. Huge numbers of people still visit Scarborough, especially during bouts of good weather in the summer, but they come by car and most of them do not stay overnight.

The tastes of the remaining visitors changed and, for example, the open-air theatre failed to attract audiences and was forced to close down. In its place was 'It's a Knock-Out'. 'Gala Land', which was the lineal descendent of the Aquarium, was also forced to close. The spa was expensively refurbished but this failed to stem the flow of the conference business away from Scarborough. Earlier, two of the town's four railway lines shut down. The closure of that which went to Whitby was a mistake by any standards. Even the herring fishing went into terminal decline. In contrast to this sad story of decline was the success of the Stephen Joseph Theatre (the former Odeon Cinema) under Alan Ayckbourn as its director and resident playwright. It shows its unmistakable origins as an inter-war cinema with touches of Art Deco.

Old Odeon Cinema, Scarborough. Unmistakably an Art Deco cinema, this building, opened in 1936 and now houses the very successful Stephen Joseph Theatre.

Literary Associations

It is not surprising that Scarborough has attracted several literary associations. In Tobias Smollett's *Humphry Clinker* (1771), his character, Matthew Bramble, gets into trouble in the sea at Scarborough but is rescued and brought ashore in such a state of deshabille that his embarrassment causes him and his party to leave town the next day. R.B. Sheridan makes the town the scenario for his comedy *A Trip to Scarborough* of 1777. Anne Brontë became a habitué of the town and died in 1849 at No. 2 The Cliff, in a house that was demolished to make way for the Grand Hotel. She did not leave the town, being buried in the detached part of St Mary's churchyard. Charlotte Brontë recorded visiting her grave in 1852.

Ann Brontë's headstone. This is to be found in the overspill burial ground close to St Mary's.

Anne Brontë was working as a governess when she first visited Scarborough, at a time when she was suffering severely with depression. In *Agnes Gray* (1847) the eponymous heroine is unhappily employed as a governess. Much of the novel is on the gloomy side, reflecting Anne's state of mind, but it is lightened by its happy ending. She is at Scarborough and she conveys her own love of the place and especially her delight in the sea:

> There was a feeling of freshness and vigour in the very streets, and when I got free of the town, when my foot was on the sands and my face towards the broad, bright bay, no language can describe the effect of the deep, clear azure of the sky and ocean, the bright morning sunshine on the semi-circular barrier of craggy cliffs surrounded by green swelling hills, and on the smooth, wide sands, and the low rocks out at sea – looking, with their clothing of weeds and moss, like little grass-grown islands – and above all, on the brilliant sparkling waves. And then the unspeakable purity and freshness of the air!

In 1887 poet Edith Sitwell was born in her family's seaside residence of Wood End, which now houses a museum of related material. She died in 1964. Osbert was born in the town in 1892 and locates his scathing attack on upper-class mores *Before the Bombardment* (1926) in the town. Charles Laughton, the actor, was born locally, as was the painter Lord Leighton.

In 1876 Atkinson Grimshaw (1836-93) moved to Scarborough with his family. It is probable that more people recognise his paintings than know who painted them or indeed anything about the man. His beautifully evocative portrayals of leafy middle-class villas in Victorian suburbs, of leafless trees on winter afternoons and of gas-lit and usually damp docksides at

The unusual three-dimensional sign outside the old Golden Ball pub on Sandside, Scarborough.

A police box, Scarborough. Developing communications technology has rendered this type of street furniture obsolete and few have survived.

places like Hull and Liverpool retain the ability to make a strong impression. He found in both Scarborough and Whitby a stunning topography which he wanted to interpret and reproduce. Examples are: Scarborough Lights (*c.*1877); Light in the Harbour, Scarborough (1879); Nightfall in the Harbour, Scarborough (1881); Baiting the Lines, Whitby (1884) and Full Tide, Whitby (1883).

There are many others.

It is difficult not to see much of Scarborough as a somewhat faded example of the decline of the English seaside resort in the last forty years. However, nothing can take away from the town's wonderful site and, a little tired and jaded as it may be, it is still a place for which large numbers of people have great affection. There may be 'kiss-me-quick' kitsch but there are also glorious sands and quiet, colourful gardens and magnificent views out to sea.

7

SCARBOROUGH TO BRIDLINGTON

Brompton

A few miles west of Scarborough on the A170 to Pickering, stands the village of Brompton. It was here that the first heavier-than-air flight took place. The year was 1853 and the man was Sir George Cayley, born in 1773. He deserves to be better-known.

At the little parish church of All Saints, William Wordsworth married his childhood sweetheart, Mary Hutchinson, on 4 October 1802. While they were celebrating their nuptials, something was afoot at the late Georgian Brompton Hall which was close by. In its grounds, the local squire, Sir George Cayley, had a shed. This was where he was designing the world's first aeroplane. His family had lived in the area for generations and he was the sixth baronet. Being rich, he had the time and the money to indulge in his interests which always involved a bent towards the sciences. When he was a mere schoolboy, he had devised a method for measuring the speed of the beating of a crow's wings and had also subjected his thumbnail to scientific scrutiny. With unerring accuracy, he managed to measure how fast it grew. Exactly half an inch in one hundred days, he concluded triumphantly. It is evident that George was something of an oddball as a boy, even if he was clearly extremely bright and resourceful.

His scientific activity gave him little time for the pursuit of the fairer sex. However, he was a highly eligible bachelor and he seems to have allowed himself, probably against his better judgement, to marry a Miss Sarah Walker from Nottingham. It was not a happy union. She resented his obsession with things scientific, feeling that he should be paying her more attention. In fact, Sir George severely taxed her limited reserves of patience and the couple took to acrimonious rowing. She was more vociferous and, cowed by her verbal assaults, he was only too keen to get away into the garden shed. This, of course, only made it worse the next time.

However, when he was in his shed he was at one with the world and by 1796 he was becoming more and more obsessed with designing what he hoped would be a flying machine capable of lifting a person off the ground. With string, whalebone and feathers, he constructed miniature ornithopters that had flapping wings and would fly for a few seconds when wound up and then released. He went on to design toy gliders, modelling them on the wings of large birds that he had studied closely. He realised that crucial to the power of flight were the two factors of forward thrust and lift.

Sir George next designed an ingenious device which replicated the forces working on the wing of a bird when it is in flight. The story goes that this was just about the last straw so far as his wife was concerned and she refused to have the device in the house, and moreover said that if he and his playmate came anywhere near her, she would not be responsible for her actions. Sir George and his wife's turbulent relationship had not been totally fruitless because she announced that she was pregnant and it was decided that she should go to her parents' home for the confinement – probably a happy course of action for all concerned.

No sooner had the carriage conveying her to Nottingham disappeared down the drive than Sir George, now free to spend the entire day indulging himself, brought his contraption inside the house and somehow got it up to the top of the stairs. He then launched it down the stairs where it flew for a short distance having achieved the lift he wanted. Thrust was still a problem but by now he was so excited that he wrote a letter to *The Times* newspaper in which he held forth lyrically on the possibilities for human aviation. His suggestion that humans one day would be able to travel in flying machines at speeds of between 20 and 100mph was met with hoots of derision.

Ever eager to bring his inventive genius to bear on new challenges, he put off his aeronautical activities for a few years. He invented a successful method of making the rifling for big naval guns. He additionally designed a powerful portable telescope; a prosthetic hand; possibly caterpillar tracks for vehicles moving across muddy terrain; a seat belt for passengers on railway trains; and a net fixed to the front of a railway locomotive which would scoop up, totally unharmed, any human or other trespasser unable to get out of the way of an approaching train. He also decided to become MP for Scarborough.

In the 1840s he returned to his first love – aeronautics. He built a triplane which carried a small boy off the ground for a few feet, admittedly after it had been launched on a slope. Finally, in 1852 he built his 'New Flyer'. He described this contraption in considerable detail in the 15 September issue of *Mechanics*. It was a monoplane with a kite-shaped wing and a tricycle undercarriage. To keep the weight down, he devised light wheels rather like those on a modern bicycle.

This machine flew for the first time in 1853. Sir George was by now seventy-one years of age and perhaps just a tad old to play the part of a test pilot. He was clearly aware of the concept of *noblesse oblige* and so he very magnanimously, even generously, volunteered his coachman John Appleby to undertake the role, but without informing him first. He felt sure that Appleby would feel highly honoured to be in the driving seat, literally, of what would be such an historic event – man's first heavier-than-air flight. When Appleby was informed of the ground-breaking nature of what he was about to do, he was less than enthusiastic. Even if the blasted contraption ever got off the ground, it was likely to plummet swiftly to earth and Appleby had no great desire for posthumous recognition as the first human flyer.

However, Sir George was the squire and his employer so with marked reluctance Appleby allowed himself to be placed in the machine. This was then launched from the side of a hill within the estate by half-a-dozen farm hands running like the blazes while pulling ropes attached to it, thereby supplying the thrust. It soared into the air, the farm hands let go and the 'New Flyer' flew at least 200 yards over a small valley before landing with a bump on the other side. Sir George was jubilant, although the unhurt but traumatised coachman-guinea pig clambered out and promptly handed in his notice.

Brompton Hall is now a school but there is a plaque, apparently visible from the road, which is on the side of the shed in which Sir George had carried out much of his design and development work.

Filey

Filey has some handsome streets of Victorian houses, a steep cliff down to its promenade which overlooks fine sands, and the reputation of being a pleasant family resort. As with so many of the settlements along this coast, Filey was originally a small fishing village and the flat-bottomed craft called cobles still go out for the daily catch.

The parish church of St Oswald is strangely placed outside today's town and provides a dramatic seamark for mariners. It has Norman, Early English and later features and a massive crossing tower. An unusual feature in the south aisle of the nave is a crude statue of a Boy Bishop.

St Oswald's, Filey. The interesting old parish church is situated where the old village used to be, some distance from the more modern part of Filey on the far side of Church Ravine.

Such representations are very rare. In some monasteries and rural parishes, it was the custom in medieval times to choose a boy to carry out the duties of bishop between St Nicholas's Day which was 6 December and Holy Innocents' Day on 28 December. During that time, the chosen boy was invested with the full authority of the bishop and had to be obeyed as such.

A memorial remembers the splendidly-named Claudius Galen Wheelhouse. He was an eminent surgeon practising mostly in Leeds but he also officiated as a churchwarden at St Oswald's for nineteen years.

Parts of the pre-Victorian settlement can be seen around the church but the town is predominantly of the nineteenth century and it enjoyed its greatest period of growth after the railway to Scarborough and Hull was opened in the mid-1840s. In 1800 the population was little more than 500 but had risen to 1,230 in 1841. Fishing, agriculture and some boat-building employed many local people but Filey set out its stall to be an elegant and select seaside watering place. Local people welcomed what they hoped would be additional income which made them less dependent on the vagaries of the sea. During the following years, six classical style stuccoed blocks were erected in the Crescent. They then, and indeed still do, impart an air of slight superiority to Filey over other Yorkshire resorts. The Crescent Hotel itself was certainly one of the best seaside hotels in England. The building of the Sea Wall and the Promenade not only had the effect of improving the sea defences but provided a place where people could walk to see and be seen. The town still has a pleasantly sedate Victorian feel, a fine beach, the lovely Crescent Gardens and an enjoyable promenade.

Filey station retains the overall roof characteristic of the stations that the North Eastern Railway built in many of the small towns it served.

The Crescent provides evidence of the pretensions of Filey to be a classy resort.

Now largely forgotten was the attempt that Filey made at being a spa. After all, both the neighbouring resorts of Bridlington and Scarborough claimed to have curative waters so it was important that those places didn't have everything their own way. The spa was at a bleak spot on the north side of Carr Naze to which genuine invalids and others – mostly hypochondriacs – made their way. Although it was said that the medicinal powers of the various springs at Filey had been known for centuries, they were only exploited in the nineteenth century. Claims were made that the waters were of great value for those suffering from rheumatism, dyspepsia and various 'nervous' disorders – all suitably vague. The impression given, however, is that the Filey Spa was all a bit half-hearted and it fizzled out by the end of the nineteenth century. The site has since gone under the sea.

The heyday of Filey as a middle-of-the-range fashionable family resort was probably in the Edwardian period. The years from 1901 to 1914, although people did not necessarily realise it at the time, marked the end of Britain's undisputed position as 'Workshop of the World' and as the nation that 'ruled the waves'. The country had recently experienced two telling blows to its perception of itself. Firstly, large numbers of young working-class men and youths who volunteered to join the Army and fight in the Boer War were rejected as unfit on medical grounds. How could this happen in the most advanced society in the world? Worse followed when the might of the British Army suffered three consecutive defeats by the Boers, who the British regarded as nothing better than boorish peasants. By the middle of the 1900s it was evident that Britain was engaged in an arms race with Germany in order to maintain her naval superiority and within a few years it became obvious that the country was heading towards war. These underlying concerns were present in spite of the appearance of a seamless transition from the Victorian to the Edwardian era.

However, in terms of real prices and the cost of living, the Edwardian era was a good one for the middle classes who had money to spare for leisure activity and recreation. They probably also had holidays with pay. There was now less emphasis on the 'rational recreation' beloved by serious Victorians and more on the pursuit of genteel and harmless pleasures. So what was on offer at Filey as an example of a fashionable resort for the middle classes and even some of the upper classes at this time?

Music was well up the list of favourites with operas, orchestral and choral concerts and, perhaps slightly more demotic, bands such as the Crescent Gardens Subscription Band giving a couple of recitals daily during the season. In 1911 the Grand Theatre opened its doors, giving the town a facility that could be used both as a theatre and a cinema. Professional and local amateur companies provided performances. Pierrots performed on the beach and sport was available for the more energetic visitors. Activities on offer included golf, foot races, hockey, cricket, football, swimming, gymnastics, athletics and cycling. Less energetic exercise could be had by strolling in the North and South Crescent Gardens. Before the First World War the beach was even used as a landing strip for the primitive aircraft of the time, there being great public interest in displays of their capabilities. Needless to say, these sorties only took place when the tide was out! The beach also proved useful for public demonstrations in which early motor cars were put through their paces.

Filey was always happy to leave most of the razzmatazz to Scarborough and Bridlington and it has continued to do so successfully, although most visitors might question the writer of

Filey Brigg. This picture shows the deep runnels scoured out by rain on the unstable boulder clay.

1806 who compared Filey favourably with the Firth of Forth near Edinburgh, with the Bay of Naples and with Constantinople!

The beach is sheltered from the north by Filey Brigg which is a finger of hard sandstone rock jutting out a mile or so to sea. It is topped with boulder clay which has been deeply scoured by channels made by rain gushing off it after storms. The boulder clay represents material scraped up by glaciers about 15,000 years ago, carried some distance and then deposited when the glaciers melted and retreated northwards. It is fertile but unstable. Sheltering Filey to the south is Flamborough Head and the bay has been created by the sea eating away at the less resistant boulder clay between the two headlands.

Local myth has it that Filey Brigg is the first part of a bridge that the Devil was building to link Yorkshire with Europe and all was going well until he dropped his hammer, whereupon he was so fed up that he went off in disgust. Another explanation for Filey Brigg's existence is that it is composed of the skeletal remains of an enormous dragon which died there. Neither explanation is very plausible. A Roman signalling station once stood on Filey Brigg. The Romans came to Filey around AD 70. Archaeologists have unearthed part of what is believed to be a Roman pier and some stones thought to have come from some kind of lighthouse they built to guard the coast. It is likely that the small settlement that was Filey at the Norman Conquest would have suffered severely when William carried out his scorched-earth policy in the north of England. It was Filey's misfortune to be by the sea when in 1085 Danes threatened an invasion and William ordered the destruction of anything along the coast that might have been of value to invaders. After this, Filey was probably little more than what was accurately if disparagingly described as 'waste'.

By the early twelfth century, it is likely that Filey was a very small community engaged in fishing and agriculture, but it is difficult to escape the conclusion that it must have grown larger and richer quite quickly in this century given that much of the fabric of the parish church of St Oswald's, a large and fine building, dates from the latter part of the century. It would have helped the settlement that it obtained a charter for a market in 1221.

Filey Brigg was the location of what was perhaps the first recorded wreck on the Yorkshire coast. This occurred in 1311. While Edward II had apparently devolved the Rights of Wreck to the Lord of the Manor of Hunmanby, in this case Richard de Lacy, this did not stop him instigating enquiries about a chest containing gold and silver coins valued at £300 which had disappeared after a wreck. The result of this enquiry is not known but in 1318 another ship was wrecked nearby, but since its only value was as salvage estimated at 40 shillings, not even the King could be bothered to get excited. In 1348 the *Katherine* ran aground close by and the records show the outrage felt by the local lord of the manor when evildoers carried away several chests full of coins. Perhaps he protested too much because the King put out a warrant for his arrest on a charge of piracy.

An estimate of the population of Filey in the first decade of the seventeenth century is 500. James I and Charles I had little interest in maritime matters and it must have been a matter of concern to local fisherfolk that the Dutch more-or-less controlled the North Sea and engaged in piracy and plunder against local vessels. It has to be said that ports elsewhere in England also sent ships to sea whose main purpose was piracy and that they were quite happy to attack ships operated by their fellow-countrymen.

Brontë Plaque. The dissipated Branwell Brontë spent time in Filey.

It may seem strange but Filey, for all its present decorum, once had the reputation of being a godless place, being described as such by none other than John Wesley. Congregations used to amuse themselves during boring sermons by flinging pieces of dried skate at the parson, or so it is said.

Filey is the southern starting point of the coastal part of the Cleveland Way which takes in some of Britain's most stunning coastal scenery on its way to Saltburn-by-the-Sea where it then goes inland.

Dr Beeching wanted to close the railway passenger service between Scarborough and Hull, a measure which could only ever have been contemplated by someone who did not use railways, and understood little or nothing about the social and economic role they continued to play even in an age of greatly increasing private car ownership. Fortunately the line through Filey did not close but was subjected to various cost-cutting exercises including de-staffing of wayside stations.

A fine museum is housed in old cottages in Queen Street and proudly displays material especially about the local fishing industry and the activities of the lifeboat service.

8

BUTLINS AT FILEY

William Edmund Heygate Colbourne Butlin was born in South Africa in 1900. He went on to become famous as Billy Butlin. He had little formal education and his father never succeeded at anything and was eventually divorced by Butlin's mother. She was involved in travelling fairgrounds and was herself itinerant, taking her son with her while she worked in South Africa, Canada and also in England.

As a child he had a formative experience. With his mother he endured a holiday in a guest house at a seaside resort in South Wales. The landlady was a virago of formidable appearance and fearsome demeanour who made being misanthropic and niggardly into art-forms. She seemingly delighted in driving her guests out onto the bleak seaside streets immediately after breakfast, irrespective of the temperature and the weather. Ringing in the ears of the woebegone guests was the instruction that on no account were they to return until half-an-hour before dinner, i.e. something like eight hours later. Dinner, like breakfast, was frugal in quantity and loathsome in quality. While Butlin was there, it apparently rained every day and all day. Even as a boy, he realised that the British seaside resorts needed to be more hospitable and to provide shelter and entertainment for holiday-makers from the seemingly incessant rain and cold.

Butlin left school at the first available opportunity and did various menial jobs around circuses and fairgrounds. He went to Skegness in Lincolnshire, on what can kindly be described as a 'bracing' part of the coast, with his mother who was running a number of stalls and side-shows. He quickly realised the simple truth that holiday-makers spent more money when it rained because they had to find somewhere to shelter. He then began to nibble around the idea of providing some kind of holiday 'experience' in which they would spend money, literally come rain or shine.

Butlin had entrepreneurial talent. When he had been in Canada he had seen dodgem cars in action. They always seemed to be popular, with their element of controlled risk and excitement, and very shrewdly he bought an exclusive franchise to operate this kind of show in the UK. He started operating dodgems in this country and they proved immensely profitable. He now had some real money and was looking to use it to make a lot more. He had a brief partnership with Warner Holidays in the provision of residential holiday camp at Hayling Island in Hampshire. The residents stayed in chalets to which they had access at all times, but they made their own entertainment. What about a holiday camp which provided similar entertainment, full catering and a programme of entertainment and activity with shelter from the elements when necessary – all at an inclusive price?

Out of this concept came Butlin's first holiday camp, which was at Skegness. It opened in 1936 and was quickly followed by another at Clacton. The timing of this initiative was particularly felicitous given the passing of legislation in 1938 giving all industrial workers a week's annual holiday with pay.

The camp at Filey opened in 1939. It had partially opened when hostilities started whereupon it was commandeered and became 'RAF Filey'. It reopened for holiday business in 1946. Butlin apparently regarded Filey as his favourite camp and he used it as a place to try out new ideas. For example, it was the first of his camps to have areas divided into 'houses' like boarding schools and to develop a sense of community by holding various competitions between them. Filey was also the camp which pioneered the idea of self-catering. This was in the late 1950s.

Filey made it into the *Guinness World Records* on account of it having what at the time was the longest bar in Britain. It was nearly 200ft long and had twenty beer fonts, stillage for thirty barrels and in full swing required the services of thirty bar staff, twenty floor waiters and ten washers-up. Also in the record book was the 'Gaiety' theatre on the camp. This had the largest auditorium in the UK with its seats all one level. There were 2,500 seats. At its height, Butlin's at Filey offered accommodation for over 10,000 campers. They were supported by 1,500 staff.

In a sense a small town in its own right, Butlin's at Filey was very labour-intensive. It had a substantial permanent workforce of plumbers, painters, electricians and other maintenance people such as gardeners. Others worked during the season only, but the numbers were huge. There were catering staff, cleaners, medical attendants, nursery nurses, clerical workers, telephonists, the immortal redcoats, organists and a range of entertainers and sports trainers. On Saturday an army of operatives employed by a firm in Hull turned up and gave the self-catering chalets a thorough clean and going-over in the shortish interval between one lot of campers vacating them and the next lot arriving. An operation like this needed to be extremely slick. There were few complaints despite the huge throughput of campers.

Among people who featured at Filey but went on to greater fame were Charlie Drake, Tommy Handley, the ITMA team and Des O'Connor. A less well-known name was Johnny O'Mahony. He spent several seasons at Filey in the role of camp 'tramp'. This involved him dressing up like Worzel Gummidge and wandering round the camp as the centre of attraction for a gaggle of children – oh what innocence! He committed suicide in the late 1970s while residing in a hostel for down and outs. Sadly, fantasy and reality seem to have come together in his case. He was the little-known brother of the late and always lugubrious and dry comedian, Dave Allen.

The publicity material stated that Butlin's camps 'offered the fun of a camp with the luxury of a hotel'. Before the Second World War, campers paid from £1.75 to £3 per day, depending on the time of the season in return for which they got accommodation and surroundings which were certainly better than many seaside boarding houses, three daily meals included and access to a huge programme of entertainment. It was relaxed and informal and the redcoats thought they weren't doing their job if anyone was looking bored or refusing to take part in the games and competitions. These were the days when people were much more prepared to muck in with strangers; the days before television, consumerism and private motoring had cut through family and community values and isolated and alienated large swathes of the population. It was classless in the sense that everyone had access to everything that was on offer, but in reality the clientele were mostly lower middle-class and skilled working-class people in regular work. They needed to be because although a huge amount was on offer for an all-in price and represented good value, taking a whole family there worked out quite expensive. Although some people could not cope with the idea that they had to have constant, enforced fun, it would not be unfair to say that Butlin did manage to make people feel like millionaires, even if it was only for a week.

Butlin was an able and astute businessman who made himself enormously wealthy but his employees mostly regarded him as a brute to work for, completely intolerant of any slackness or incompetence. He was totally opposed to union membership among his workforce and conditions of employment were poor. However, there was never any shortage of applicants for employment as redcoats, despite the poor pay, the long working day and the long season away from home from which no break was allowed. Those who applied probably saw it as a way into a showbusiness career and when their application form came through the post, they received an information pack in which it said: 'A redcoat is an individual, a character, a personality, a sporting type, a sing-song leader, a bingo caller, a children's uncle, a dancer, but above all – a mixer, a mingler.' Those who received this information could have no doubt then on what they were letting themselves in for.

Although these camps started before the war, it was Butlin's good fortune to develop them in the euphoria immediately following the war when people consciously wanted to put the bad times behind them and go out and enjoy themselves. In the heady days of rising real wages and full employment in the post-war boom of the 1950s and early 60s, they had the money to do so.

Butlin's camps provided a huge source of inspiration for satirical writers and cartoonists. It was probably unhelpful that the senior manager at each camp was known as the 'camp commandant' with its sinister undertones of concentration camps. The word 'camp' did not perhaps have quite the same connotations then. Totally unsubstantiated rumours used to circulate that campers were not allowed out to savour the bright lights of Filey, but it was the proud boast of Butlin's that there was everything on hand in the camp that any holiday-maker could possibly want. Other rumours did the rounds about people being forced to have fun and feeling totally humiliated if it was evident that they were not. These rumours were clearly picked up by senior management at Butlin's and taken seriously which was why they came up with the immortal slogan for one of their camps: 'Don't, please don't, think you've got to be gay at Prestatyn.' The English language of course is constantly changing and at the time such a statement wouldn't even have raised a titter or an eyebrow.

Filey had a funfair, beauty contests, glamorous granny competitions, talent shows, bonny baby contests, knobbly-knees contests, donkey derbys, concerts, floor shows, and competitive sports. Something was going on all the time. Kindergartens provided supervised activities for the children while their parents perhaps enjoyed a drink at one of the many bars scattered around the complex. Coach trips to notable places nearby were organised, as were rambles. The latter were so closely supervised that it seemed as if Butlin's were worried that the participants, having sampled life outside the camp, might get a taste for it and make a bid for freedom. There was something for absolutely everyone except those who wanted a quiet, sedentary kind of holiday.

Meals were taken in huge, hanger-like dining rooms which could accommodate hundreds of people at each sitting. As the camper ate, the tannoy kept up a constant barrage of jollification, or inanity, depending on your point of view. Examples could be, 'Legs eleven, what a smasher! Two fried eggs and a gammon rasher,' or 'How do you want your cornflakes? Fried or boiled?' Here is a typical day's provender from 1960:

BREAKFAST
grapefruit, bacon and eggs, bread and butter,
marmalade, tea.

LUNCH
roast leg of lamb, mint sauce, beans, roast and boiled potatoes,
bread and butter, fruit tart and custard.

TEA
brown and white bread and butter, jam and cakes.

DINNER
soup, steamed salmon and cucumber, vegetables,
blancmange, cheese board.

No silly nonsense about calories and cholesterol there, then.

The camp even had resident Church of England and Roman Catholic priests and on Sunday mornings makeshift churches were rigged up in two of the bars for those wanting to worship. Several babies were christened each year during the season at Filey. No statistical data is available about the number of babies legitimately or illicitly conceived between sheets in the chalets, but it is a fact that hundreds of romances started every year at Butlin's, Filey. A godsend for publicity purposes was the affair that started one year at Filey between a Miss Pott and a Mr Kettle and which culminated a year later in their marriage.

By the 1970s, tastes were changing and what really did for the Butlin's concept was the growth of cheap overseas package holidays by air to places where warm, sunny weather was almost guaranteed. Of course, many of the amenities and facilities at Filey were under cover but even Billy Butlin himself could do little when a sea fret swept in and inevitably took some of the jollity out of proceedings. It could possibly have been anticipated, but the terse announcement at the end of the 1983 season that Filey was to close with immediate effect still came as a surprise.

It's time to leave Butlin's at Filey but at least let's bow out in an upbeat fashion by recalling the rousing reveille over the tannoy that welcomed the dawn and jolted campers out of their slumbers at quarter to eight every morning, without fail. It was entitled 'Good Morning, Campers' and here are two sample verses:

Roll out of bed in the morning
With a great big smile and a Good Morning –
Wake up with a grin,
There's a good day tumbling in!

Wake up with the sun and the rooster,
Cock-a-doodle-do like the rooster use'ter
How can you go wrong
If you roll out of bed with a song?

The day could only get better after that.

For boys and girls aged 6 to under 9
This is your own special programme–
please detach

BEAVER CLUB

Sunday

MORNING

9.00 Roller Skating on the Rink

10.00 to 12.30 The Amusement Park is open. Free rides for all

11.30 Junior Who's Who and Beaver Club. Come along and hear all about this famous Club. Children's Theatre

AFTERNOON

2.00 The Amusement Park is open. Free rides for all

2.00 Roller Skating on the Rink

2.30 The Wild West. Come dressed as a Cowboy or Indian. There's a prize for the best dress. Meet at the Children's Theatre

3.00 Grand Welcome Party. A special invitation from Uncle Ron to all parents and children. Meet your Redcoats in the Princes Ballroom

4.30 Picture of Health Competition for children 3 to under 6 in swimwear in the Princes Ballroom

EVENING

6.30 to 8.00 Merry Go Round. The Amusement Park is open with selected rides specially for you

7.00 to 8.00 Happy-Daze with Uncle Ron in the Children's Theatre

7.30 to 8.30 Enrol for Swimming Instruction with Sacha in the Indoor Pool

8.15 to 9.00 Cartoon Films in the Children's Theatre

Goodnight children — see you in the morning

Monday

MORNING

9.00 Roller Skating on the Rink

10.00 to 12.30 The Amusement Park is open. Free rides for all

10.15 Junior Miss. Competition for girls 6 to under 9 years, wear a pretty dress in the Princes Ballroom

10.15 to 11.15 Introduction to Floor Gymnastics: Leotards, shorts or swimwear must be worn, 6 to 8 years in the 913 Club

10.30 Mr Bounce Hopper Eliminations. Sponsored by Corgi Toys, on the Sports Field

11.00 Captain Blood Chase. Meet in the Children's Theatre dressed as a pirate to seek out the wicked Captain Blood! Prizes for the best costumes

12.00 to 1.00 Trampoline Fun in the 913 Club

AFTERNOON

2.00 The Amusement Park is open. Free rides for all

2.00 Roller Skating on the Rink

2.15 Beaver Band Parade. Bring an instrument (paper & comb or anything) for a Grand Parade. Meet at the Children's Theatre

2.15 to 3.15 Floor Gymnastics in the 913 Club

2.30 Dad & Lad Competition for boys 3 to under 9 years. In the Princes Ballroom

3.30 Family Sports Meeting with events for Beavers. On the Sports Field

4.30 The Peanut Street Gang present **Humpty Dumpty** (Part One) in the Children's Theatre

EVENING

7.15 to 8.30 Cartoons in the Children's Theatre

8.30 to 9.30 Uncle Rons Showtime in the Children's Theatre

Tuesday

MORNING

9.00 Roller Skating on the Rink

10.00 to 12.30 The Amusement Park is open. Free rides for all

10.15 Cadbury's Mother & Child Contest for children over 3 to under 9 years. Sponsored by **Cadbury's Fudge.** In the Princes Ballroom

10.15 to 11.15 Floor Gymnastics in the 913 Club

10.30 Mr Bounce Hopper Final. Sponsored by **Corgi Toys.** On the Sports Field

11.00 Beaver Bingo, it's free and just for fun in the Children's Theatre

AFTERNOON

2.00 The Amusement Park is now open. Free rides for all

2.00 Roller Skating on the Rink

2.15 to 3.15 Floor Gymnastics in the 913 Club

3.00 to 4.30 Make A Paper Hat (Bring Newspaper) then join the Disney Parade. Meet in the Children's Theatre

3.30 to 4.00 Junior Circus Time. Cycling in the Princes Ballroom

4.30 The Peanut Street Gang present **Humpty Dumpty** (Part Two) in the Children's Theatre

EVENING

6.30 to 8.00 Merry Go Round. The Amusement Park is open with selected rides specially for you

7.15 to 8.30 Cartoons in the Children's Theatre

8.30 to 9.30 The Peanut Street Gang present **Haunted House** in the Children's Theatre

Goodnight children — see you all in the morning

Butlins Beaver Club
Membership of the Club is free. Badges can be purchased for 20p

In order to keep the little darlings occupied and give their parents some rest, there was a continuous all-day programme of activities under the 'Butlin Beavers Club' umbrella.

A Butlin Beavers Club badge. In the days when small boys in particular liked to encrust themselves in enamel badges, this was a much sought-after one.

A very unusual feature of Butlin's, Filey, was the opening of its own railway station in 1947. This had long platforms, albeit with little in the way of shelter, to handle the many special trains that ran on summer Saturdays to and from the camp. These came from as far afield as London and Scotland. The station was at the apex of a triangle which allowed trains to branch off the line from Scarborough to Bridlington and approach the camp from both the northerly and southerly directions.

Bempton Cliffs

Accessible only on foot, Bempton Cliffs are some 400ft high and from spring to mid-summer attract vast numbers of nesting sea birds. An RSPB reserve contains fenced viewing terraces from which the birds can be observed safely. Among the species which regularly breed at Bempton are kittiwakes, guillemots, razorbills, puffins and gannets. Few sights equal that of a gannet plunging like a lethal arrow 100ft or more into the sea in pursuit of its piscine prey. Bempton is the only location on the British mainland where gannets nest.

A popular spectacle used to be the egg-climbers or 'climmers' as they were known. They were local men who risked sudden and violent death by using ropes to move around on these fearsome cliffs, taking eggs from birds nestling precisely in the kind of nooks and crannies where they should have been secure from human predators. This unpleasant practice was outlawed in 1954. The eggs were sold locally or taken to Leeds where the whites were used in the manufacture of leather.

Flamborough Head

This spectacular headland juts out to sea at a maximum height of about 170ft and is made of chalk, much of which has been eroded by the sea's action as can be seen by the wave-cut platforms at the base of the cliff. The area abounds with good footpaths and is an excellent place for viewing seabirds. It has an 85ft-high lighthouse sending a beam of light 29 miles. An interesting relic is that of Yorkshire's oldest lighthouse. It was built in 1674 of chalk and is octagonal and has four storeys. It is actually the only remaining intact coal-fired lighthouse. The chalk here is much tougher than that found in Kent and Sussex, for example. An interesting collapsed cave feature known as the Pigeon Hole may be viewed. There are many caves which can only be approached by boat. Some rejoice in names such as St George's Hole, Smuggler's Cave and Robin Lythe's Hole (he was a local smuggler). It was Flamborough Head which featured in the little-known novel by R.D. Blackmore called *Mary Anerley*. The principal character was brought up on this coast and becomes a smuggler.

Flamborough Head is much visited and has its fair share of gift shops and cafés. It is actually cut off from the mainland by a mighty earthwork known as Dane's Dyke. It dates back well before this coast attracted the attentions of Danish invaders and is probably of the fifth or sixth century AD. It is thought to have been created to give Flamborough Head a defensive capability against forces attacking it from the landward direction. Even today it forms an impressive barrier with a bank over 18ft high in places and a west-facing ditch 60ft wide. Flint arrowheads found in it suggest human habitation in the area at least 2,000 years ago.

In 1779 a fight took place out at sea off Flamborough between the American privateer, John Paul Jones (1747-92), who was actually born overlooking the Solway Firth in Scotland, and two naval vessels providing escort for a convoy of merchant ships making for Hull. The engagement took place on a brilliantly moonlit night and crowds turned out to watch with a mixture of fascination and fear because they had heard that Jones was nothing more than a piratical cut-throat

The Old Lighthouse at Flamborough. This is made of chalk rubble and was erected in 1674. It went out of use in 1806.

Looking north to Flamborough Head.

who loved putting defenceless women and children to the sword. What would happen if he won the engagement and chose to land? In fact he was a seaman of the highest order and the bloodthirsty reputation that he had was what would now be called adverse spin. He had been forced to leave Scotland after killing a mutinous seaman and, already an experienced mariner, he fled to join the infant American Navy engaged in fighting the Royal Navy during the War of Independence. He managed to obtain command of *Ranger*, a fast eighteen-gun sloop with a brief to harry enemy commerce on the English side of the Atlantic. This he did to great effect, hence the stories that circulated about him. Cutting a long story short, that is how he came to be off Flamborough. During the battle he captured HMS *Serapis*, a forty-four-gun frigate, much more powerful than any of the ships in the small squadron commanded by Jones. Filey, not far away, has a bar called 'Bonhommes' after the *Bonhomme Richard*, the vessel commanded by Jones in the battle off Flamborough.

The parish church of St Oswald at Flamborough is a hotch-potch of work of different centuries. Perhaps its greatest glory is its fifteenth-century screen surmounted by a roodloft, a feature extremely rare in Yorkshire. The screen has delicate carvings of foliage and traces of its original bold colouring, and some people believe that it was brought from Bridlington Priory. Not far from the church are scanty remains of what seems to have been a small castle. It is on record that it gained its licence to crenellate in 1351. It is likely to have belonged to the Constable family, several of whom are buried and have memorials in St Oswald's. One of the memorials is unusually grisly. On the tomb of Sir Marmaduke Constable, who died in 1520, is the upper part of a skeleton; in the rib-cage can be seen his heart. On the heart is a lump which supposedly represents the toad which he accidentally swallowed while taking a drink of water. It would be difficult to say who was more put out by this contretemps, but the toad is said to have made its feelings known by gnawing away at Sir Marmaduke's heart, killing him.

In a circular pit near Flamborough, a girl named Jenny Gallows is supposed to have committed suicide in the nineteenth century. Locals believed that anyone who ran nine times round the pit would hear the fairies.

9

BRIDLINGTON

Bridlington is almost three towns in one: the old town around the ancient priory church, about a mile inland; the harbour area with many fishing and other small boats, protected by two piers; and the popular resort and seafront above a fine sandy beach and alongside the north cliff.

The priory belonged to the Augustinian Order and was founded about 1120. It is the centrepiece of what is known as the 'Old Town' with narrow streets and a feeling of antiquity. Following the Dissolution of the Monasteries in 1539, much of the priory church was pulled down and the remainder became the parish church. Even in its truncated, mutilated form, it is an impressive building. Close by is the High Street with its attractive old bow-fronted buildings and the spacious Market Street where the priory had possessed a charter allowing it to hold markets and occasional fairs. A museum of local antiquities is housed in the priory gatehouse.

The priory was once second only to York Minster among all the religious establishments of Yorkshire. It originated with the Augustinian canons about 1120 and the church part of the complex was known to have been 333ft long. Much of the eastern part was pulled down along with virtually all the conventual buildings at the Dissolution. We are left basically with the nave and aisles and the two west towers as well as the gatehouse, known as the Bailgate. Oddly, part of the cloisters has been re-erected. Its last prior was foolish enough to join the Pilgrimage of Grace in 1536 as a protest against the threat of the Dissolution and he was executed for his temerity. One oddity in the priory is a little collection of carved items salvaged from the building when it was complete. These include a slab of black marble incised with a representation of a church which bears a singular resemblance to the church depicted in the Bayeux Tapestry.

In the fourteenth century Prior John gained some favourable publicity when, during a storm in the bay, he performed a miracle by apparently walking across the waves and rescuing the crew of a ship in distress by single-handedly towing the vessel into the harbour.

'The Quay' is how the area around the harbour is known. A harbour existed as early as 1113 but the structures that can now be seen date from the nineteenth century and provide shelter for a sizeable fleet of inshore fishing boats and also a variety of pleasure craft. The Bridlington Harbour Heritage Museum traces the history of local fishing and Bridlington's maritime history. Cobles are available for those who want to do a spot of deep-sea fishing.

Bridlington Priory Gatehouse. This gatehouse (known as the Bailgate) was built in about 1390. The upper parts were rebuilt in the seventeenth and eighteenth centuries. This building has been used as a prison, a Non-conformist place of worship, a barracks, a school and a museum.

Sea conditions in early February 1871 were so bad that collier and other ships were assembled in huge numbers in the Tyne waiting for the weather to abate. A break in the conditions meant that no fewer than 400 of them set sail on 9 February, only for the weather to turn even worse on the morning of 10 February. Five vessels were out of control and approaching the coast in mountainous seas. Bridlington had two lifeboats but one could not be controlled in the turbulent seas and the other, *Harbinger*, was left to do its best. The next morning the beach was piled high with timber washed ashore from the cargo of wrecked ships. At least ten vessels were destroyed. Probably as many as seventy lives were lost in twenty-four hours and at least forty-three were washed ashore and buried in a mass grave at the priory. They are remembered in an annual service and by a memorial.

Queen's House stands above the harbour and is thought to stand on the site in which Henrietta Maria took refuge when a fleet of ships supporting the Parliamentary cause bombarded the town from the sea. She had just returned from Holland where she had managed to obtain money and military supplies to support her husband, the King. This was clearly a scary experience and she wrote to the King telling him how she had not liked the music made by cannonballs as they whistled through the air, not far above where she was sheltering.

Bridlington began to attract a few visitors in the late eighteenth century. They were mostly well-to-do and came largely to bathe on the fine beach, to dance and to perambulate. Hot and cold water baths were available for those who did not trust themselves in the sea. Bridlington's real development as a seaside town began after the railway arrived in the 1840s. Street after street of substantial terrace houses, some used as residences but most as guest houses, were built between 1850 and 1880 to give Bridlington the very Victorian feel this part of the town has. Dominating all was the ornate and prestigious Alexandra Hotel of 1866 with some Italianate and French Renaissance motifs. This is evidence that Bridlington was continuing to set out its stall to attract a semi-exclusive clientele. This former icon of Bridlington's semi-exclusive past was demolished in 1975 and a high and wholly out of scale block of flats was built on the site.

It was while she stayed nearby at Easton House Farm that Charlotte Brontë and her friend Ellen Nussey decided to walk to Bridlington in 1839. This walk provided her with her first ever sight of the sea, which was a deeply emotional experience. She was so affected by her first sight of the German Ocean that apparently she had to shed a few tears before she could bring herself to speak. She obviously recovered her equilibrium because she went on to say, 'The idea of seeing the sea – of being near it – watching its changes by sunrise, sunset – moonlight – and noonday – in calm – perhaps in storm – fills and satisfies the mind.' The experience also meant that she had had to sit down, her legs becoming weak as a result of her emotional outpourings. Mrs Elizabeth Gaskell, in her biography of Charlotte, says that she was 'quite overpowered, she could not speak until she had shed a few tears ... for the remainder of the day she was very quiet, subdued and exhausted'. She then stayed at Bridlington for a few days and returned in 1849 for the funeral of her sister Anne at Scarborough.

The most conspicuous feature of Bridlington Priory from a distance is this prominent tower.

In her grief she found some solace in writing her novel *Shirley* while staying at Easton House.

The railway had opened up access to Bridlington and enabled day-trippers from the West Riding and the North Midlands to enjoy a brief bout of littoral escapism. Bridlington found itself in the same situation as various other seaside resorts with aspirations to be classy. The local businessmen did not want to kill the goose that laid the golden egg. The problem was the issue of whether the goose was the 'superior', well-heeled visitor or the less well-off working people in their larger numbers. To be too snooty would deter the proletariat; to be too demotic would put off the patricians. They were on the horns of a dilemma. It seems that they found a way through this moral and material maze. In 1858 an assessment was made that 'Bridlington attracts numbers of that class of visitor for whom Hornsea is too quiet and Scarborough too gay'. Even today, Bridlington stands in a slightly uncertain position in the pantheon of English seaside resorts because it is nowhere near as brash as Blackpool or Southend although it seems to want to emulate them in some ways. Nor is it as composed as nearby Filey.

The kinds of entertainment which Bridlington offered its visitors before the First World War included donkey rides, Punch and Judy shows, Pierrots, hurdy-gurdy men, performing animals such as dancing bears, brass bands, bowling, concerts, revues, simply strolling along the prom' or sitting and watching the world go by, and excursions to local places of interest. These simple

The seafront at Bridlington, north of the harbour.

Punch cartoon 'By the sad sea waves'.
Landlady (who has just presented her weekly
bill): 'I 'ope, ma'am, as you find the bracing
hair agrees with you ma'am, and your good
gentleman, ma'am!'
Lady: 'Oh yes, our appetites are wonderfully
improved! For instance at home we only
eat two loaves a day, and I find from your
account, that we can manage eight!'
(Landlady feels uncomfortable).

pleasures were not very different from those offered at many other sizeable seaside resorts but they seem to have lacked the glitz to be found at unashamedly working-class resorts such as Clacton, Southend or Margate. In fact if a cartoon from *Punch* magazine is anything to go by, it seems that there was some needle at Bridlington between the well-off and the lower class visitors. It is called 'Galloping Snobs by the Seaside' and shows what are clearly 'society' visitors galloping on the sands and endangering the lives and limbs – and even the sand castles – of the large numbers of working-class holiday-makers disporting themselves on the beach.

Sewerby Hall is a Georgian mansion housing an art gallery and museum which includes items relating to the early female aviator Amy Johnson (1903-41) who was born at Hull.

In 1657 a local Quaker by the name of Robert Fowler started building a ship by the harbour. He did not let the fact that he knew nothing about shipbuilding get in his way. When it was complete, he and eleven other Quakers went on board and set sail for the American colonies where they hoped to establish a new and better life for themselves. They were all totally clueless about marine navigation and the story is that they made landfall on the American coast only a couple of miles away from where they had intended. They put this happy chance down to the power of prayer.

That lugubrious northern comedian, the late Les Dawson, appearing one year at a summer show at Bridlington, found it hard to engage with the audience. His comment was, 'You could see the dampness rising from the wet raincoats like mist on the marshes.'

10

BRIDLINGTON TO HULL

The lofty cliffs that have been such a feature of the coast from the mouth of the Tees give way after Bridlington to a very different kind of coastline. The coast and the terrain inland are low and flat. The cliffs are puny and are being rapidly eaten away by the relentless encroachments of the sea and the land peters out at the bleak and ill-frequented Spurn Head. Westwards to Hull are the low cliffs and sands of the north bank of the Humber Estuary. Hull itself is 22 miles from the open sea on the impressive estuary of the Humber.

Tourists largely pass this coast by. The reality is that from Bridlington to Spurn Head there are something like 40 miles of almost disregarded, unspectacular, often lonely coast with sandy beaches to die for. The north bank of the Humber east from Hull, much of it reclaimed land, only attracts the occasional birdwatcher.

Carnaby

Carnaby is a small village nearly 3 miles inland from Bridlington on the A166. North-west of the village stands Carnaby Temple, a well-known architectural folly. It was built by one of the Strickland family from nearby Boynton Hall in 1770 and designed as an eccentric version of the ancient Temple of the Winds in Athens. It is brick-built with two stories and is surmounted by a domed roof and an octagonal lantern. It is, and must always have been, supremely useless. This is precisely why it is delightful and must not be allowed to fall down. Actually follies do have a use/value if they gave pleasure to the people who built them and pleasure to subsequent generations who like an eye-catcher or simply enjoy quirky buildings. To be fair to Carnaby Temple, the Home Guard used it as a look-out during the Second World War.

The Stricklands were known for their eccentricity and nearby St Andrew's Church contains an eccentric lectern. Whereas the flat part of a lectern is usually supported by the outspread wings of an eagle, this one has a turkey as its supporter. There is a reason. This unprepossessing and singularly gormless bird was introduced into England by Sir William Strickland.

Rudston

Rudston is a small village standing a few miles inland from Bridlington on the B1253 road, but worth mentioning because the churchyard contains Britain's tallest standing stone at 25ft 9ins and thought once to have been nearer 28ft. The existence of this monolith in a churchyard served to tell us that this site was considered sacred long before the Christians established a church here. In fact, experts think that the stone was probably erected 2,500 years before Christianity began to make an impact on these islands. It is made of grey gritstone thought to have been dragged to Rudston from the nearest outcrop, which is at Cayton Bay about 10 miles away. Christians often adopted pagan sacred sites either in respect for the awe in which they were held or in an attempt, not always wholly successful, to destroy any remaining pagan sentiments. The mystery is the question as to why the Christians, once they felt fully in control, did not demolish the stone. Legend has it that the Devil was very angry that a church was being built in this spot so he hurled the monolith at it in an attempt to destroy it. Obviously his aim wasn't too good. I think we can discount this story as the monolith was obviously there before the church.

Rudston Monolith – the tallest standing stone in Britain.

Burton Agnes Hall

Just to the south-west of Bridlington stands the village of Burton Agnes with its well-known hall. This is a beautiful early Jacobean house with ghostly associations. It is haunted by a particularly gruesome spectre by the name of 'Awd Nance'. Hers is a sad story. The youngest of three sisters, Anne Griffiths grew up at the hall as it was being built and she loved it. One day, returning from a visit to friends, she was set upon by a gang of footpads and left fatally injured. Five days later she died, but not before having issued her family with the rather sinister instructions that unless her head was interred within the house she loved so much, her ghost would make life in the hall extremely unpleasant for all who resided there.

Her relations thought that this bizarre wish was evidence that Anne's mind was deranged and they went ahead and buried her intact in the churchyard close to the hall. No sooner had this happened than the hall at night-time was rendered unbearable by inexplicable sounds as if angry crowds, bent on revenge, were running screaming and shouting hither and thither throughout the house. It was impossible to tolerate these disturbances and so her relations arranged to have her body disinterred. To their horror, they found that her head had now become detached and that even after such a short time, it quite simply resembled a fleshless skull. The body on the other hand showed no sign of mortification. Reluctantly, the relations took the vicar's advice that the skull be brought into the house. As soon as they did so, the unwelcome happenings ceased. Subsequent occupiers of the house occasionally decided to get rid of the grisly relic that came with the place. Yes, you've guessed it. As soon as it was removed, the disturbing phenomena manifested themselves once more. As soon as it was returned, all was serenity and peace. Now the skull resides in the hall and all is well, except that occasionally the ghost of Anne is seen flitting around the house as if she is checking to ensure that its present occupants are looking after it with a due amount of love and reverence.

Skipsea

This is an unremarkable place full of caravan sites but notable because of the remains of its castle. As readers will have noted, there aren't many castles along the Yorkshire coast. This was a motte and bailey of considerable size and even today, after centuries of erosion, the motte is over 40ft high. The castle was certainly in existence by 1086 and had been built by Drogo de Bevere who was a vassal of William of Normandy. He sounds a nasty piece of work because in 1086 he was banished from the kingdom for murdering his wife. The castle was destroyed by order of Henry III in 1221. It is cared for by English Heritage and is freely accessible. An unusual feature of the castle was that the motte was separated from its bailey by an area of marshy ground known as Skipsea Lake, which presumably acted as a defensive barrier. It also provided a supply of eels.

The coast is eroding quickly in the neighbourhood and an adjacent village, Cleeton, went under the waves many years ago.

Hornsea

Hornsea is a quiet and sedate resort, very much off the beaten track, which still displays some of the buildings appropriate to its old role as a market town. Close by is Hornsea Mere which is 2 miles long and Yorkshire's largest freshwater lake, popular for boating and fishing. It fills a depression in the boulder clay and is filling up quite quickly. The Hornsey Pottery attracts substantial numbers of visitors. It produces a distinctive brown-glazed pottery and started in 1949. In the main street is the North Holderness Museum of Village Life, which is open in the summer.

Hornsea became a select watering place in the late eighteenth century when three chalybeate springs were discovered and people made their way there to take the waters for their health's sake. A stage coach service from Hull started in 1821 and a railway opened up in 1864. A Hull timber merchant by the name of Joseph Wade decided to make a speculative investment in the development of a select watering place that would combine the role of a spa with that of a seaside resort. These aspirations were only partially realised and the town now sees trippers in the season, and commuters and retired folk all the year round. Hornsea never took off in a big way and it suffered when the railway line closed in 1964 as part of the ill-considered 'Beeching Cuts'. At least Hornsea station remains in situ, being listed as of special architectural or historic interest.

On Willow Drive opposite the museum stands Bettison's Folly. This is a brick-built tower 50ft high with a castellated top; a fine example of a venture by someone with more money than sense. The builder was Mr W. Bettison and it was built in 1844 so that his servants could climb up it and get advanced warning that their master's carriage was in sight. They then informed the kitchen staff, who made sure that dinner was served promptly on his arrival. The tower has a corrugated appearance because of the use of reject burnt bricks, known locally as honey bricks, which protrude from its walls.

About 2 miles west of Hornsea on the side of the B1244 is Mushroom Cottage. This is a strange little circular building.

Aldbrough

Aldbrough is a little inland (much less than it used to be) and provides excellent visual evidence of coastal erosion as the lanes going east towards the sea end abruptly at the edge of very low cliffs, of what seems little better than mud, where pieces of the last buildings to be abandoned can be seen sometimes, standing crazily halfway over the edge. They do not stay there for ever; usually they disappear into the sea with the next really powerful storm. The coast is retreating at well over 10ft annually.

A less spectacular stretch of coastline than those we have already surveyed, much of this is taken up with the flat land of Holderness. This may be somewhat obscure and unvisited by today's standards but it reveals the hand of man in earlier times by its superb parish churches, which are evidence of the medieval prosperity of the area. Holderness terminates at the shifting peninsula of lonely and slightly spooky Spurn Head, where material that has been eroded from further up the coast is constantly being deposited.

A few miles south of Aldbrough, a short distance from the shore, is Grimston Garth. This is a strange triangular house built in the 1780s at a time when buildings of this sort were enjoying an understandably short-lived vogue. It is built in the mock-Gothic style fashionable at the time.

Withernsea

This faded small seaside resort has a lighthouse and a curious castellated gateway which now leads nowhere but was once part of the pier (the pier built in 1875 and long since been demolished). Withernsea became a watering place with the arrival of the railway from Hull in 1854. Before that it was a hamlet with a population of no more than 109 people. There were ambitious plans to turn Withernsea into a major seaside resort and a 'Withernsea Pier, Promenade, Gas and General Improvement Company' was established in 1871, under the auspices of a Hull businessman called Bannister. As with Hornsea, the great aspirations were never realised and a guidebook of 1890 described the resort as, 'a dreary watering place' – a trifle uncharitably, perhaps. The railway line from Hull closed in 1964.

For those who like their seaside without the razzmatazz, Withernsea ticks all the boxes. An oddity is the lighthouse in its very central position in the town. The lighthouse became disused in 1976 and now contains a museum combining material about the history of the town with information about the RNLI.

Legend has it that there were once two foolish sisters who wanted to build a church for the village. One was determined that the church should have a tower only, while the other was just as adamant that it must have a spire. They fell out over the matter and huffily decided that, since they couldn't cooperate, they would each build a church in close proximity. St Margaret's became a ruin early in the seventeenth century while St Peter's was washed away by the sea in 1816. Thus passeth earthly glory.

Kilnsea

If anyone needs confirmation of the rate of coastal erosion in these parts, they need go no further than the tiny settlement of Kilnsea. A small building in the village states that it was built in 1847 and was then 534 yards from the sea. It is now only about 200 yards. The strip of land on which Kilnsea stands is so narrow that it has two shorelines. One faces the open North Sea; the other the more sheltered muddy and sandy shore and brackish marshy ground of the Humber Estuary.

Spurn Head

Spurn Head, Spurn Point or Spurn Spit is a narrow and bleak spit of sand and shingle which has been built up as the result of the coastal drift of material from further up the coast, which has been deposited here when it meets the strong currents at the mouth of the Humber Estuary which themselves bring down much silt. It is approximately 3 miles long and in places only around 50 yards wide and it is breached from time to time when it is stormy. It would have undoubtedly resolved itself into a number of small islands had it not been for artificial coastal defence works. Near the southerly end there is a now-closed lighthouse and the station from which the Humber pilots operate, every ship entering the Humber's unpredictable waters needing to take on a pilot. It is evidence of the dangerous waters where the mighty Humber meets the sea that moored, ready for action, is a lifeboat with a full-time crew, the only one in the UK. The former Spurn Lightship is now moored in Hull Marina. This vessel was unique in being painted black instead of the normal red. This was because the special atmospheric conditions at Spurn Head could make it difficult to see at times.

A lonely, probably unlovable but strongly atmospheric, point, one always gets the feeling that Spurn Spit could disappear altogether before long. Those who seem to enjoy it most are birdwatchers and the birds they come to watch. The extremity of Spurn Head belongs to the Yorkshire Naturalists' Trust.

For centuries, cobbles and gravel were removed from Spurn Head to be used as building material for houses and also in the making of roads. Spurn Head has always been a fragile environment but perhaps those who took away materials from the vicinity in the early days did not do so with the single-minded ruthlessness that characterised their later successors. By the middle of the nineteenth century, however, material was being removed in quantities sufficient to lead to breaches of the spit on several occasions. The constant movement of men, horses and wagons wore down the marram grass which basically bound the spit together. This brought conflict between those extracting material and other bodies, especially the Admiralty concerned about the implications for navigation in the area. After many decades of wrangling, alternative sources made Spurn Head less important and extraction ceased in the early nineteenth century.

Lighthouses of the Yorkshire Coast

There are several lighthouses along the Yorkshire coast. There used to be more. Here something will be said about lighthouses in general before going on to look at individual examples along the Yorkshire coast.

Ever since man first sailed the sea, he has looked for ways of aiding navigation and especially of guiding ships clear of hazards at sea such as reefs and shallows as well as dangerous lee shores. By day well-known features might be visible, such as a particular headland or distinctive church steeple. By night, however, or in poor visibility, the mariner is at a severe disadvantage without artificial lights to help him. These lights had to be reliable and always in the same designated places.

The Romans moved extensively round the world and we know that they built two lighthouses facing each other across the Straits of Dover. One was at Boulogne, the other at Dover itself. The latter of course still exists. It is within the precincts of the vast Dover Castle and is known as the Pharos. It is the oldest lighthouse in the world.

In medieval times, few guiding lights were employed. Those that did operate were often in the hands of the Church. One operated on Spurn Head, probably evidence of the importance accorded to the shipping that went in and out of the Humber in those faraway days. Occasionally, a prominent church tower would display a light in it and among these was the tower of St Botolph's Church at Boston, better known as 'Boston Stump'. All these lights were extinguished at the Dissolution of the Monasteries and Britain's coast was left literally in the dark.

The earliest lights established after this period seem to have been at North Shields about 1540 and Tynemouth about 1550, both presumably to assist navigation into the busy River Tyne. However, the building of lighthouses along the British coast was a slow process. In 1700 there seem to have been just eleven and these were all along the east or south coasts.

Trinity House was established in 1514 to control and lay down a code of practice for the pilots who were needed to navigate ships in difficult waters, especially around river estuaries. In 1836 it assumed responsibility additionally for lighthouses, lightships, navigational buoys and so on. From 1870 to 1900 it was responsible for the building of a large number of lighthouses. The intention was to cover the entire coast systematically with lighthouses at intervals of no more than approximately 20 miles; so from seaward, shipping would always have at least two lights within visual range.

The world's first lightship was stationed at The Nore which is at the entrance to the Thames off the Kent Coast. This was in 1732 and was a piece of private enterprise, financed by tolls from passing ships. Trinity House assumed control of lightships and at one time there were about thirty. Most of these were at places of particular navigational importance along the east coast.

The basic source of light in medieval lighthouses was a fire burning wood, peat, reeds or coal in an iron brazier. In that sense it was a beacon. The danger from fire led to experiments with alternative sources of fuel such as candles and oil lamps but coal became the standard fuel until electricity developed as a practical proposition in the nineteenth century.

Now we will look at some of the lighthouses that have done their duty along the Yorkshire coast. The Humber Estuary has always been difficult to navigate because of sandbanks which constantly change their shape and position. Dredgers need to be working constantly to keep a channel clear. The lighthouse at Spurn Head, which came into use in 1428, was probably the first lighthouse since the Pharos at Dover, mentioned earlier. It was maintained by a public-minded hermit by the name of Richard Reedbarrow. His worthy effort was swept away in a huge storm and unfortunately he went with it. A second tower was erected in 1678 and was expensive to maintain because it was difficult to get coal to this remote spot. A number of lighthouses succeeded this but many succumbed to storm damage. The present light was erected in 1895 and is 120ft high. Close by is the stump of one of its predecessors. For many years there was also a light ship anchored in the Humber, close to the tip of Spurn Head.

Withernsea lighthouse stands in the town and was set up in 1894 to assist ships entering the Humber and to keep them away from Bridlington Bay. Flamborough has a particularly imposing lighthouse which was established originally in 1806 standing 214ft high on Flamborough Head, which itself is 200ft high. Scarborough has a dinky little lighthouse down on the harbour quay. This does not really signal to ships out at sea but shows lights which indicate to the fishing and other craft which use the harbour what the depth of water is, and other navigational information. The present lighthouse is a replacement for the one destroyed by German shelling in 1914.

Just down the coast from Whitby and high on the cliff-top at Ling Hill is Whitby lighthouse. This was established in 1858 and the current lighthouse dates from 1890. Down on the harbour piers are two beacons which look similar to scaled-down lighthouses but, like the light at Scarborough, not only provide navigational lights but show fixed lights indicating the depth of water available at the harbour entrance.

The next major lighthouse up the coast is at Roker Pier, Sunderland.

Patrington

This village is not on the coast but is only a short distance inland and is mentioned because of the size and outstanding beauty of its church, which contains some of the finest features of the so-called Decorated period to be found anywhere in Britain.

The size of its church is indicative that this was a very prosperous medieval community, almost certainly based on sheep-rearing. One thing that makes Patrington St Patrick's so remarkable is its unusual architectural uniformity. It was begun at the end of the thirteenth century and its spire was completed about fifty years later. It is a textbook of the Decorated style of architecture and it is probably the richness of the architecture, plus the happy proportions, which make this such a rewarding building. There are delicate carvings everywhere and a rare surviving Easter Sepulchre. This is located on the north side of the altar, usually in the sanctuary. In it the Blessed Sacrament or Host was placed from Good Friday to early on Easter Sunday when it

St Patrick's, Patrington, which is a superb example of ecclesiastical architecture of the so-called Decorated period of the fourteenth century.

was returned to the latter amidst considerable ceremony. On it there is a carving depicting the Resurrection and above it the Ascension. There are over 200 carved heads peering down from the arcades and the roof.

A short distance south is Patrington Haven, which was once a port of some substance but whose trade was killed off by land reclamation in the vicinity and it finally petered out in the late 1860s.

Paull

This tiny place, with expansive views up the Humber to Hull and across it to Immingham, has a small, disused lighthouse which came into operation in 1836. The place is rather dominated by the nearby chemical works and the vast tankers and crude carriers associated with it.

A curious story is told about a nearby farmhouse called Paull Holme. Some time around 1500 a terrified bull is said to have rushed through the door, charged up the stairs and leapt from a parapet, landed unscathed and then continued to hurtle off into the great blue yonder. All that was needed was a cock crowing and then we would have had a complete story.

Hedon

Hedon was at one time the major port of this part of England but its access to deep water silted up, there was a massive fire in 1656, and Hull took over its role. Hedon enjoyed access to the Humber via a canalised inlet called Hedon Haven, which was rather on the narrow side.

This magnificent church at Hedon is known as 'The King of Holderness'. It is convincing evidence of the former importance and wealth of the town.

The town was built to a geometrical grid pattern within the confines of a square boundary ditch and enjoyed much success for a period through its trade in wool and hides. It had three churches and half a mile of harbour frontage divided between three docks. At the start of the thirteenth century Hedon ranked eleventh on the list of English ports, but its days as a port were numbered. By 1476 two of its churches had fallen into disuse.

However, its prosperous past is evident in its Church of St Augustine, the only one of its churches that has survived but an absolutely magnificent one. It is a huge edifice of almost cathedral-like proportions looming over the redbrick Georgian terraces characteristic of the town and it was once much larger. Not for nothing has it been referred to as 'The King of Holderness'. Its main features are a massive central tower of the Perpendicular style, an earlier chancel and transepts, and what is often described as a gothic gem which is its thirteenth-century font. The aisles to the transepts and also the Lady Chapel have gone.

Hedon has an air of departed glory. Because it has not grown significantly, it largely retains its ancient street pattern. There is a town hall which contains a superb civic mace of the early fifteenth century, believed to be the oldest of its kind in England.

II

KINGSTON-UPON-HULL

This city, somewhat off the beaten track and commonly known as Hull, stands on the small River Hull which flows into the Humber at this point. The town developed on the west bank of the Hull in the area still known as the Old Town, which retains its medieval street plan and has many fascinating old buildings. Hull was, and indeed still is, a major seaport and the docks stretched along the waterfront for several miles. Some of them, including that which is now Queen's Gardens, have been filled in. The activities around whaling ceased long ago while there is little, if any, fishing left. As late as the 1940s more fish were landed at Hull than anywhere else in Britain, even including Grimsby. Industries associated with fishing were formerly huge employers in the city.

Hull was once derisively described as 'a fish dock on the end of a branch line'. Its comparative remoteness has caused it to have something of an insular attitude which even the building of the Humber Bridge has not altogether broken. It would be true to say that Hull is not a fashionable place, although many people brought up in the city have a fierce loyalty to it. The bridge itself is beautiful. It was a long time in coming, many people arguing that there was no unassailable economic case to be made for building it. However, it opened in 1981 and had the longest single span of any bridge in the world. For those who like statistics, the bridge contains cables with a total length of 44,000 miles – far more than the circumference of the planet Earth. The bridge replaced a ferry across the Humber to New Holland which, because of the difficult tides and shifting sands of the Humber, often had to make a very indirect crossing of the river. A curiosity of the Corporation Pier, from which the ferry plied to New Holland on the Lincolnshire shore, was that it had a railway station, owned by the Great Central Railway, but it never saw any trains. It was one of only two such stations in Britain, the other being Dartmouth. They had every facility to be expected of a railway station, except rails and trains, both of them being served only by railway company-owned ferries.

The town that grew to be Kingston-upon-Hull began its life with the bluntly uncompromising name of Wyke. It was a little port established at the confluence of the River Hull with the Humber Estuary by the monks of Meaux Abbey during the third quarter of the twelfth century. Clearly these Cistercian monks may have had their spiritual side but they also had a keen material awareness, and an eye for the main chance when it came to making a bob or two. Wyke was a planned medieval town with a grid pattern of streets alongside the River Hull which the monks straightened and canalised. Wyke exported the agricultural produce of its East Riding hinterland, most notably wool, and built up a successful trade, particularly importing wine and salt. The Cistercians did very well out of all of this. In 1293 the manor containing Wyke was bought by Edward I, who went on to improve the port facilities in what became known as Kingston-upon-Hull (i.e. King's Town). He enlarged the quay, established a mint, extended the markets and fairs and improved the roads to and from York and Beverley.

Extra incentives for merchants to settle here arrived in 1299, when the townspeople were given their first borough charter and freedom from tolls throughout the kingdom by Edward I. During the following century, Hull flourished and it acquired a unique and distinctive townscape. The burgesses ringed their town with a massive towered wall and erected an enormous church – and did much of this in brick, a building medium which had been almost totally ignored since Roman times. There was no town wall along the River Hull and no quay either. Because of this, an Act of 1558 decreed that Hull was the only town in England where ships were allowed to load and unload away from a quayside. This privilege was as much prized by Hull merchants as it was disliked by customs officials. Smugglers were very pleased.

Before this, in 1541, Henry VIII had graced Hull with his presence along with the then love of his life, Catherine Howard. They dropped in unexpectedly but the town's burghers put on such a good show that the King showed his gratitude by unbuckling his belt and presenting the Mayor with his sword. The sword is still part of the civic regalia.

Access to the ships on the Hull was by the narrow passages which still run down to it from the High Street. They are known as staithes, perhaps because there was once some kind of wharf or loading place at the end of each lane. By the middle of the fourteenth century almost every space within this tight girdle of walls was packed with dwellings and commercial premises, and the fruits of royal patronage were obvious. Most successful towns owe much to their home-grown entrepreneurs and Hull was no exception, producing the de la Pole brothers who were probably the most affluent and perceptive speculators and money-lenders in the kingdom. The family dynasty dominated the town for much of the fourteenth century. Yet such good fortune could not protect Hull from the effects of wider forces. As the Hanseatic League of northern trading ports expanded its influence, so the merchants of Hull found themselves barred from the Baltic ports and, in the second half of the fifteenth century, Hull entered a deep recession. The Hanseatic League took over the cloth trade and preferred trading with London.

The town stagnated and even by the middle of the sixteenth century, it had failed to expand beyond the confines of its walls and there were even empty plots within the walls. During the sixteenth century, there were some signs that Hull was beginning to prosper again. Profitable trade was started with Russia and the Baltic ports around the time that the Hanseatic League was in decline. Much of the production of the West Riding woollen industry was shipped through Hull. Corn and flax, pitch, tar and timber in particular entered Hull in the reverse direction. When Daniel Defoe visited the town in 1700, the area within the walls was becoming extremely congested. He found it serving also as an outlet for Derbyshire lead and butter, cheese from Cheshire and the Midlands and, when harvests were good, corn from Yorkshire and the North Midlands. He fulsomely praised what he saw as the honesty of the

Hull merchants. Defoe made Hull the point of departure for the voyage in which his fictional hero Robinson Crusoe was stranded on a desert island.

Before its recovery began Hull had witnessed dramatic events in 1642 when Charles I found himself on the end of a very different kind of reception from that accorded to Henry VIII. It would not be unfair to say that Charles lacked sound judgement. He also had the arrogance which went with his belief in the divine right of kings and knew that in the town there was an arsenal containing military munitions which he was anxious to get his hands on. He knew that the supporters of Parliament were equally bent on securing this materiel. Anyway, the King in his purblind way felt certain that the citizens of Hull would not only welcome him with joy but happily hand the supplies over to him as well. To his disgust, 23 April 1642 proved to be just one of those days. With several hundred supporters, Charles rode to Hull from Beverley only to find the town gates secured against him. This was aggravating because he had been expecting to dine with the town's governor, Sir John Hotham. Hotham appeared on the battlements and blurted out apologetically that, on the instructions of Parliament, he could not open the gates. He begged the King's forgiveness for

Charles I at Hull. In April 1642, Sir John Hotham at Hull, under instructions from Parliament, refused the demand of Charles I that he be given entry to the city.

the way things had turned out but it was more than his job was worth, etcetera, etcetera. The King commanded, the King wheedled, the King begged but Hotham remained apologetically obdurate. The King thought that time might break Hotham's resolution so he waited for five hours. Hotham himself waited patiently but time did not soften his determination. The King had little option but to turn round and ride back to Beverley, his tail between his legs. Hull was the first place openly to rebel against the King.

The Baltic trade was recovered and as well as handling imports from the Baltic, Hull was also shipping in wine, oil and fruit from France and Spain, and tobacco and sugar from the West Indies. However, there was a fear that the town was vulnerable to bombardment from the sea and that its excessively crammed nature within the walls could be a real problem in the event of fire.

In the eighteenth century, Hull's prosperity continued virtually unabated and its population increased sixfold, which necessitated tearing down the town walls in order to find the space for new docks. By the end of the century, Hull ranked fourth in the list of British ports behind the much larger towns of London, Bristol and Liverpool. Hull's fortunes continued to grow with the rise of the West Riding woollen industry and the whaling trade. By this time, the River Hull was lined with the kind of brick-built warehouses found in so many other similar locations. The cranes in these buildings extended outwards sufficiently to load and unload directly into and from the ships on the river.

Trinity House, Hull. Trinity House was built in 1753 and originally housed a school for the sons of mariners. The school still operates.

Although Hull acquired docks from 1775 onwards, the High Street complex remained active and little altered until the Second World War. Bombs did much damage and the stupidities of post-war so-called town planning wreaked more destruction until wiser counsels prevailed and it was realised that the area was one of great historic interest. Now a few warehouses remain, given over to other purposes, and a handful of the wealthy town houses that were once such a feature of the area. These include Wilberforce House and Maister House – which is generally reckoned to have the finest Georgian staircase outside London. By 1800 Hull was the third busiest port in Britain after London and Liverpool.

The Church of Holy Trinity has a noble tower which somehow manages to maintain a dignity and serenity among the nondescript clutter which is much of Hull's city centre. It stands close to the Market Place on the west side of Hull's Old Town and its position and size show how central a place it had in the days of medieval Hull, and also what a prosperous place

An old street close to Holy Trinity Church in the centre of Hull.

Hull was. This church has work of the Decorated and Perpendicular styles, which is of the very highest quality. There are fine memorials of the de la Pole family.

The de la Poles are recorded at Hull as collectors of Customs on behalf of the Crown as early as the fourteenth century. The family went on to become Dukes of Suffolk and for some time one of the most powerful dynasties in England. It is likely that involvement with Customs provided many opportunities for enrichment, even peculation. The area around Hull witnessed much 'owling' or illegal smuggling out of wool in the fifteenth century. An official investigation revealed that shady businessmen from York and Beverley used the many small and lonely creeks on the north bank of the Humber to load wool, thereby avoiding paying duties in the official port of Hull. In 1698 it was estimated that over 120,000 packs of wool were illegally shipped out of the Hull area. Shortly afterwards Hull was provided with its own revenue protection vessel called the *Humber*. However, given that it had the job of patrolling the entire area between Flamborough Head and Ingoldmells, just north of Skegness in Lincolnshire, it would have had its work cut out to stem the tide of inward and outward contraband. It didn't help that the commander of the vessel considered it to be a hopelessly slow vessel, woefully lacking manoeuvrability.

Occasionally a smuggler turned gamekeeper. In 1745 a Captain Joseph Cockburn gave evidence to a Parliamentary Committee enquiring into smuggling. He commanded a Customs cutter based at Boston in Lincolnshire but admitted that he had learned the ropes at sea, literally, aboard a smuggling vessel working the Kentish ports. He described how, in 1738, just one smuggling trip had earned him a profit of no less than 250 per cent. This had involved picking up 2,040 gallons of brandy at Dunkirk and sailing with it into the Humber where it was transferred to a keel, a flat-bottomed boat of a type extensively used on the rivers of Yorkshire. The keel then carried its precious cargo inland up the River Trent. He told the Committee that smuggling was rife on the Humber because it was so simple – there was no effective preventive service.

In the 1760s a great variety of goods were seized by the preventive men around Hull and the Humber, although what they managed to impound would only have been a small proportion of the total of free trade activities in the area. The range of commodities they impounded was quite amazing. They included salt, starch, soap, candles, spices, medicines, vinegar, paper and more bizarre items such as human hair (for use by wig-makers), musical instruments and playing cards. These commodities have little in common with the popular perception of smuggled goods – the brandies and gins, perfumes and French frilly silk knickers!

In the Ferens Art Gallery, Queen Victoria Square, there are many artistic depictions of Hull's maritime past. Close by, also in Queen Victoria Square, is the Maritime Museum with strong sections on whaling, the fishing industry and the city's history as a port. It is housed in the former Docks Authority office. The Maritime Museum exhibits many examples of scrimshaw. It has the best collection in the world. During their off-duty hours, the crew who manned the whaling ships would carve walrus tusks, or the teeth of whales, with various designs and motifs. These would either be sold or kept as souvenirs. Either way, good pieces of scrimshaw now command a high price when they come on the market. Sometimes the crew of whalers would be given part of their wages in the form of whalebone, or the teeth of whales, because these had what would now be described as 'street value'.

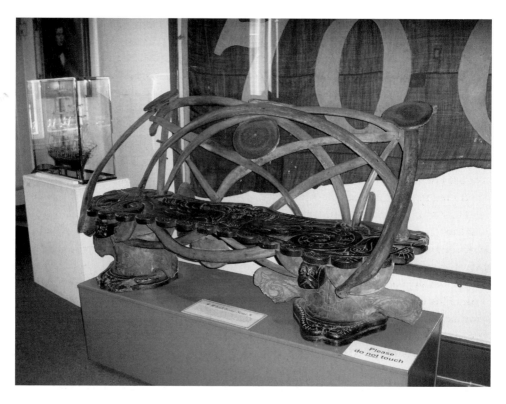

In the Maritime Museum at Hull are many reminders of the former whaling industry. They include this chair made of whalebone.

The poet Andrew Marvell (1621-78) spent his childhood at the vicarage attached to Holy Trinity Church and attended the grammar school presided over by his father, who drowned in the Humber in 1641. Marvell was three times Mayor of Hull and a statue commemorating him stands at the corner of Savile Street and George Street.

The poet and novelist known as Stevie Smith (1902-71) was born in Hull, although she left the city at the age of five. Her best-known work is probably 'Not Waving But Drowning' (1975). Other local people to have made an impact include the dramatists Alan Plater and John Godber and the actors John Alderton, Ian Carmichael, Tom Courtenay and Maureen Lipman. J. Arthur Rank (1888-1972), the movie giant, and Amy Johnson (1903-41), the pioneer female aviator, are other locals to have left a permanent impression. The poet Philip Larkin (1922-85) was not a native but spent much of his working life as librarian at the University of Hull. He called Hull a frightful dump. It's not as bad as that.

The Humber is truly a mighty river where it flows past Hull. Into the Humber pour the waters of most of Yorkshire's rivers. The bigger ones are the Swale and the Ure, which unite to form the Yorkshire Ouse and also the Nidd, the Wharfe, the Aire, the Calder and the Don. It also receives the waters of the Trent, the third longest river in Britain. This rises as far away as

Biddulph Moor in Staffordshire and drains much of the Midlands. All these rivers were more or less navigable at various times in the past and York and Doncaster, for example, were at one time significant inland ports. As the English economy and those of its trading partners developed in early modern times, so ships became bigger. Long, slow, uncertain voyages in increasingly large vessels up rivers subject to flooding, silting or both, became less practical. Hull benefited as a place where transhipment into sea-going ships took place, with a cut for the local merchants and ship-owners, of course. The days of ports as far inland as York were numbered. Hull, on the other hand, prospered as a port. Britain's industrial development stimulated a demand for imported raw materials and for the export of manufactured products. Hull was ideally placed to be a major port for trade to Northern Europe. There was also considerable engagement with the coasting trade.

A Dock Company was formed in the 1770s and the first dock, later Queen's Dock, was completed in 1778. It was on the site of old fortifications. It was only the fourth wet dock in Britain and by far the largest when it was built. Hull went on to have 239 acres of enclosed docks and a very long waterfront. A large proportion of the city's working population was employed in shipping, the docks, transport, and industries processing imported raw materials. In 1911 Hull was the third largest British port and although the North European trade remained dominant, ships arrived from and departed for most quarters of the globe. Most of the docks were owned by the North Eastern and Hull & Barnsley Railway Companies and the city had a railway network of considerable complexity. Hull's peak as a commercial port was reached in the early 1960s. Its main trade then was in timber, grain, oil seeds, petrol, wool and fruit. A decline set in but Hull continues as a container port and international ferry terminal.

Hull still contains reminders of its industrial past, most of which reflected the city's importance as a port. By the Drypool Bridge over the River Hull stands this gaunt former flour mill which, in the autumn of 2009, appeared to be awaiting conversion to offices or apartments.

Its significance as an industrial centre and port meant that Hull attracted large-scale bombing during the Second World War. The distinctive configurations of Spurn Head and the Humber Estuary virtually guided enemy aircraft to the place. Large parts of the centre were destroyed and rebuilt post-war, at a time when British architecture was at a nadir, a legacy which Hull is working to replace.

Hull does not have a romantic image. Even its name is abrupt and uncompromising. However, it is well worth a visit, not least because of its superb collection of municipal museums, the river frontage, the large numbers of ancient buildings around the Old Town and the area around Holy Trinity Church. In the High Street stands the house in which William Wilberforce was born. He was a leading campaigner against the evils of slavery while at the same time being one of the most vehement opponents of reforms in factory conditions in Britain. On display in this house are manacles, branding irons and two appalling whips, used to chastise fractious slaves. One is of rhinoceros hide and the other, no less than 7ft long, is formed out of twisted and compacted grass.

A very different and more recent attraction is The Deep. This rears up rather threateningly on the waterfront overlooking the Humber but it offers superb entertainment and education for those who wish to acquaint themselves with the denizens of the world's oceans. They are

Land of Green Ginger, Hull. Although this is certainly one of the most fascinating street names in the UK, there are many theories and little agreement as to how it originated.

The Deep, Hull.

a wonderfully diverse lot and it is possible, for example, to eyeball a man-eating shark with complete safety.

On the Boulevard stands the statue of Skipper Smith. His right arm is held aloft as if he is gesticulating. If he was, it didn't do him much good. He was a Hull trawlerman engaged with others in the everyday task of fishing the North Sea – in this case off the Dogger Bank. Everything was going as normal one day in 1904 until Russian warships turned up and without warning started firing on them. They inflicted much damage on the unarmed fishing vessels and George 'Skipper' Smith was one of two fatalities. Incredibly, the whole tragic episode was a case of mistaken identity – on the part of the Imperial Russian Navy. They were at war with Japan at the time and identified the trawlers as Japanese torpedo boats and so, taking no chances, bombarded them.

Hull was in the thick of things again during the 'Cod Wars' of 1958, 1972 and 1975. The coastal waters around Iceland offer some of the richest deep-sea fishing in the world. Access to the fishing grounds there excited hostility, as far back as the 1890s, between the Danish who then controlled those waters and British vessels. These were resented by the Danes because the large British steam-powered trawlers were able to scoop up what they thought of as unfairly large catches. Incidents occurred where trawling gear would be cut adrift or confiscated and both nations, and later the Icelanders themselves, had to resort to armed naval vessels to defend

Arctic Corsair. This floating museum is an ocean-going trawler moored permanently in the River Hull.

First-time visitors to Hull are always surprised by the colour of its telephone boxes. They are reminders of a former municipal enterprise when the city operated its own telephone system. This box is a K6 of the sort that could be found in their thousands right across the UK, although it is distinctive not only for its colour but also because Hull boxes lack the crown above the door found in boxes elsewhere.

the interests of their respective fishing fleets. The actual 'Cod Wars' were brought about when Iceland unilaterally, if understandably, extended its territorial waters from 4 miles to 12, to 50 and eventually 200 miles. Although the politicians negotiated agreements, the access to the fishing stocks for British ships became so limited that many Hull trawlers were forced out of business and the 'Cod Wars' were therefore a major contributor to the decline of Hull as a fishing port.

Moored in the old port area just inside the River Hull is the Arctic Corsair. She was involved in the fracas with Iceland in the 1970s and has been beautifully restored as a floating museum of, and tribute to, the brave men and hardy vessels that sailed out of Hull in search of the fish.

12

THE WHALING INDUSTRY

One industry always associated with Hull was the Greenland whaling industry. It is said that the first ship to sail out of Hull in search of the Arctic whale did so in 1598. From this small beginning Hull became the greatest whaling port in the world. When the whale was virtually exterminated in the northern hemisphere, Hull turned from processing blubber and whale oil to producing oil by seed-crushing and the processing of other primary products.

By 1613 ships from England, the Netherlands, France and Flanders were hunting the whale in the waters around Greenland and Spitsbergen and each bitterly disputed the others' right to be there. At first the legal right for British whaling was awarded to the Muscovy Company, but illegal free-lancers operated as well. However, the early years of the British whaling industry seem to have been remarkably amateurish and incompetent, and our rivals were doing much more successfully, especially the Dutch.

The ships used in the early days had a displacement of about 200 tons, were strongly built – as indeed they needed to be – were rather slow and not particularly manoeuvrable. They had steeply sloping sides or tumblehome to withstand the pressure of pack ice. They carried a crew of anything from twenty-five to fifty. These included skilled harpooners, coopers and cutters who had the particularly repulsive job of preparing the whale-flesh for boiling. The whaling voyage started in March and the main quarry was the right whale, but other whales were taken, as well as seals – the fur of which was particularly prized.

The method of hunting the whale (always referred to as a 'fish') was extremely hazardous. On sighting the whale, a flotilla of small row-boats would set off in pursuit with the harpooner poised on the prow. The harpoon was like a long heavy arrow and it was attached to at least 30ft of high quality, extremely strong rope. The extreme danger of the job lay in the need to approach the whale closely enough for the harpoon to penetrate deeply into the monster creature which, in terrible pain and fear, then thrashed about with its tail, the flukes of which were quite capable of smashing a small boat to smithereens along with all those in it. A virtuoso harpoonist was a man who could dictate his own wages. Having been struck, the whale soon plunged but not before the men would attempt to get more lines into it. A trial of strength and endurance followed, the puny boats in danger of being capsized and their occupants hanging on like grim death hoping that the whale's strength would be exhausted. As it began to weaken, other boats would close in for the kill. All the boats would then combine their efforts to tow the whale back to the mother-ship.

The carcase of the immense creature was then 'flensed' or cut up, and the fat or blubber was stored in barrels. Much of the skeletal structure would be kept, including the jawbones and teeth because they had a market value. The work involved was filthy and repulsive and the men worked quickly because as soon as the whale started to decompose, it gave off a scarcely imaginable repulsive stench.

The whole mission was fraught with hazards. The seas in the hunting grounds were among the most dangerous in the world. Icebergs were a menace and it was not unknown for whaling ships to get trapped in the ice and crushed to matchwood in spite of their sturdy construction. Even if the ship was not crushed it might be unable to move, food supplies would run out and the crew would starve. Men injured themselves and lost limbs through gangrene and frostbite. Sometimes men literally froze to death. Occasionally ships returned empty-handed, having been unable to locate the whales.

Once returned to port after a successful voyage, the blubber was rendered down to turn it into oil in a 'blubberhouse'. These tended to be some distance from habitation because of the loathsome smell produced by the process. The whale oil was very valuable, being used in lamps for illumination purposes and also as a lubricant. Whales and seals were merrily slaughtered without a thought to the future. The right whale was the main quarry but the only parts with commercial value were the blubber, the baleen from the mouth, and parts of the bony structure – the rest was left for the killer whales, the polar bears and other scavengers. The odd-looking narwhals, which rendered up nothing other than their ivory tusks, were also killed.

After a fitful start in the whaling industry, the British grew in ability and confidence in the mid-eighteenth century. Hull and Whitby were both deeply involved in the trade with Leith and Dundee in Scotland providing competition. Britain and her rivals were saturating the hunting grounds and in 1772 one Whitby whaler noted another forty whaling vessels in the hunting grounds. On another memorable day in 1772, whalers caught twenty-seven whales between them. This kind of thing was obviously overkill but for a while it did mean that the whaling industry was making a huge contribution to the economy of Hull and Whitby. By the early nineteenth century, British whalers were feeling confident enough to attack and even capture rival vessels of the hated Dutch. However, they were operating on borrowed time. The development of manufactured gas from coal to produce cheap lighting, first for public places and then for domestic and industrial users, meant that the government bounty that whale oil attracted for the same purpose was withdrawn. This quickly rendered whaling unprofitable. It did not help that whalebone went out of fashion as a vital item in women's clothing. Whaling from Whitby ceased in 1837, from Hull soon after.

Many fascinating items relating to the whaling industry may be viewed in the Maritime Museum in Hull.

13

SMUGGLING ON THE YORKSHIRE COAST

Smuggling was, and is, a criminal activity. Most people think of the heyday of smuggling as being the period 1700 to 1850. It has been invested with a curiously romantic aura, something for which people like John Meade Falkner and Rudyard Kipling are partly responsible. It was the latter in the 'Smugglers' Song' of 1906 who celebrated smugglers as 'gentlemen' with their:

> Five and twenty ponies
> Trotting through the dark –
> Brandy for the Parson,
> 'Baccy for the Clerk.

In this chapter we will consider the general nature of smuggling during the eighteenth and nineteenth centuries and then look at the history of the trade along the coast from Scarborough to Spurn Head. Examples of smuggling in other parts of Yorkshire have been considered at appropriate places on the journey southwards down the coast.

If it is possible to call 1700 to 1850 'the Golden Age of Smuggling', it has to be said that it was not so prevalent at that time simply by chance. Successive governments in this period desperately sought to raise revenue, frequently for the purpose of financing wars, by imposing duties on imported goods, by no means exclusively of a luxury nature. The duty added considerably to the retail price. This obviously created a demand for smuggled goods available for sale at what, in effect, were significantly discounted prices. The smuggler was in business. Tea, for which there was an insatiable demand in England, might sell at 3p a pound on the Continent but would find a ready market at 25p a pound in England. No wonder smuggling became big business. In 1783 it was estimated that 50,000 British people derived their entire income from smuggling and possibly an additional ¼ million engaged in it on a part-time basis. At that time it was thought that approaching 4 million gallons of spirits were imported illegally in addition to 1¼ million pounds of tobacco and between 5 and 6 million pounds of tea. Innumerable other commodities featured in the 'free trade'.

Customs and Excise were actually different taxes. Customs had been levied for centuries and were regarded as a perk of the Crown which made a levy on all imported goods. Excise was more recent and was originally devised to help pay for the cost of the Civil War. Customs and Excise were two separate services often jealous of or even hostile to the other's activities. On occasion both services could call on the assistance of the militia or, more occasionally, of the Royal Navy. Again both services had small armed vessels and there were limited numbers of 'riding officers' whose activities were land-based, particularly patrolling the coast.

The ordinary population did not distinguish between Customs and Excise – they just resented being hit in the pocket. Avoidance of import and export duties had been going on since time immemorial but it underwent a qualitative and quantitative change in the eighteenth century. Before, it had been small-scale and essentially casual. Now the stakes were raised. It became a highly organised and capitalised industry moving huge amounts of contraband and accruing vast profits for the criminal entrepreneurs who invested in it. Smuggling was a massive criminal enterprise, in many ways anticipating the sophisticated but ruthless gangs that operated in the USA during the period of Prohibition. Virtually the entire population of England was involved. The English had become obsessed by tea and it was believed that about 80 per cent of the tea drunk was smuggled. It helped that successive governments were never prepared to invest sufficiently in the manpower and the systems needed to counter smuggling effectively. Attempts to staunch the flow on imported contraband were partial and largely ineffective.

Along the Yorkshire coast it could be argued that everyone was a smuggler. Men who worked on the land close to the sea might give up a few nights a year to help land the cargo and to carry bootleg goods inland. They would probably earn more from half-a-dozen such nights than from their labouring work over the rest of the year. They were referred to as tub-carriers. Local farmers would lend horses and wagons for transport and be handsomely rewarded for doing so. Local fishermen who knew the coast well might ferry the goods from a ship moored in deep water offshore and bring it into some suitable landing place. The ship carrying the contraband might be run up onto the beach or a convenient jetty and it might well be a local vessel manned by local mariners. Some well-armed local roughs would be employed to deter any strangers or nosy-parkers and, if necessary, to take on any revenue men or patrolling soldiers who appeared in the area. Some would guard the smuggled goods. They were known as bat-men. Even those who otherwise took no active part in a smuggling run might, for example, provide a hiding place for contraband. Everyone would get money for playing their part in the run which by necessity was a complex, planned operation. Everyone locally as consumers would enjoy the cheaper prices of smuggled tea or other items. Smuggling was an industry vital to the local economy. In hard times, the income from two or three smuggling runs a year might stave off hardship or dire poverty. It is hardly surprising that the men of the preventive service were hated. At best, when they made enquiries of local people they were met with a wall of silence or misleading information. At worst, they might be set upon, especially if they tried to arrest local people who were smugglers. It was not unknown for them to die in the course of their duties.

Before what might be described as the age of professional smuggling, finance was often raised by a consortium of boat-owners from the coastal communities who simply filled a small

One of the spots around Flamborough Head frequented by smugglers.

ship with commodities for which they thought there would be a demand in one of the north European ports. They would sail into a French or Dutch port, for example, and then barter their cargo for items they knew would fetch a good price back in England. As the potential profits from smuggling operations grew, so did the scale of organisation and the money invested in such ventures. Little information exists since those engaged in the 'free trade' prudently did not leave account books, but it is likely that the necessary initial investment was increasingly put up by businessmen in such places as London. They may well have been apparently respectable figures in society who made sure they did not deal with the 'hands-on' parts of the operation and they would remain anonymous while all the other aspects of the trade would be managed by intermediaries. They would get their disproportionately large share of the profits when the goods had been sold. It is clear that minute attention to detail was essential in an operation that might involve hundreds of people. With so much money at stake, the business partners needed to be sure that no one was engaging in their own free trade and so enforcers would be employed to mete out retribution if needed.

Often an agent was employed full-time in the foreign port to buy contraband goods, to store them and then have them available for quick loading when the ship arrived from England. A little-known aspect of the operation was the need to break down contraband into packages of manageable size. Legitimate spirits were normally kept in casks containing anything from 50 to 140 gallons. These were far too big to handle without normal quayside facilities and so gin or brandy, for example, would be decanted into casks small enough to be easily manhandled. These were called 'tubs' and were usually half-ankers holding just over 4 gallons. Tobacco and tea were much lighter but were broken down into bales small enough for one man to move. They were wrapped in oilskin and made virtually watertight. If a smuggling operation was intercepted, such containers could be jettisoned and would stay afloat for a considerable time, hopefully to be collected later or to be washed up on a nearby beach. To fool the revenue men, ingenious efforts were made to disguise items of contraband. Tobacco, for example, was made into what looked like rope usually good enough to stand up to pretty close scrutiny. Casks were manufactured with false bottoms and topped with water or wine, since the latter paid much less duty.

As smuggling became increasingly professional, so the ships used were often purpose-built. Such vessels were fore-and-aft rigged which made them highly manoeuvrable, even in difficult sea conditions. They were carvel-built, which meant that each plank making up the hull was flush against the next one, giving them extra speed through the water. Also they were often made of timber from the fir-tree which was not only cheap but light, helping to give them the edge over pursuing vessels. Such ships were well-armed and prepared to resist those trying to apprehend them. The consortia involved in professional smuggling were prepared to invest heavily, in the knowledge of generous returns if all went well. A ship that could out-sail and outgun revenue or naval vessels was therefore a sound investment.

It was stated earlier that minute planning and attention to detail were essential for every part of a smuggling operation. The bringing of a ship onto exactly the right spot on a dangerous piece of coast in stormy weather and the blackest of nights required seamanship of the very highest order. The assembling of the landing party needed to be co-ordinated with the arrival of the ship because speed and secrecy were usually of the absolute essence but it might be no easy matter in unpredictable sea conditions. There was always the chance that revenue men would turn up unexpectedly in the vicinity and last-minute changes of plan might need to be made. This often meant that a number of alternative landing points would be identified. Communication between ship and shore was essential and specialised lights were often used for this purpose. One such was a 'spout-lantern' which focussed a narrow but powerful beam of light through a long, narrow spout. This made it difficult to see, even for someone not far from the user.

The everyday expression 'on the spot' derives from smuggling and referred originally to the exact point at which the landing of the contraband was to take place. The landing would only occur when 'the coast was clear'; smuggling practice thereby giving another vernacular phrase to the rich fabric of English idiomatic expression.

Although the preventive service was overstretched, preparations always needed to be made in case their men turned up. If a customs patrol consisted of just three or four men, there was little they could do except to back off in the face of superior numbers of smugglers and especially of their bat-men. The revenue men were not well-paid and could often be bribed to turn a blind eye. There were, however, some brave and incorruptible preventive men who gave up their lives in the cause of revenue-protection. As various crimes associated with smuggling became capital offences, the poor old preventive men found their difficult job made even more dangerous. Smugglers, only too aware that they faced the death penalty if convicted, naturally saw no reason why they should not take every step to evade arrest, including murder. It is a measure of the sophistication of the smuggling industry at this time that some gangs employed

Smuggling on the Yorkshire coast. Bringing contraband goods ashore was known as 'making a run'.

surgeons to tend any of their operatives who were injured and even lawyers who specialised in defending those smugglers brought to court. Few smugglers were executed or transported. A practical commutation of a capital sentence was for the miscreant to be pressed into the service of the Royal Navy, where such men were made welcome because the majority were seasoned mariners, skilled and resourceful. Many rose to be petty officers.

Not everyone who had a horse or a wagon necessarily wanted to lend it to the smugglers or allow a barn to be used to hide the contraband even in return for payment. Occasionally someone might want to curry favour with the authorities by informing them about smuggling activity. People who did not want to co-operate, or who were suspect in any way, would be systematically intimidated. Their livestock would unaccountably become ill or a hayrick might catch fire equally mysteriously. Physical violence might be handed out and even murders were not unknown. This is a side of smuggling that people like Kipling chose to ignore.

As a smuggler, it was essential not to be caught in possession of contraband goods and therefore having a secure hiding place near the coast was essential. The coast abounds in stories about smugglers' tunnels, but in reality few ever existed. Caves were used occasionally. There were ingeniously hidden pits, perhaps in a piece of woodland, and plenty of use was made of barns and farm outbuildings. Contraband might be hidden under piles of wood or stone. Stories about the use of church crypts and bone-holes or charnel houses are probably apocryphal. In practice the smugglers wanted to get the goods on the market as soon as possible to realise their profit from the venture. The smuggled goods often needed to be converted in such a way that they could not be distinguished from the genuine article. Smuggled tobacco, for example, would be mixed with leaf from a legitimate source. Tea was broken down into smaller packets and often adulterated with dried leaves from other plants while spirits, which were usually imported over-proof, would be diluted to an acceptable strength.

Various pieces of legislation were passed in the eighteenth century in an attempt to control the growth of smuggling. In 1718 the Hovering Act made it illegal for small vessels to wait within 6 miles of the shore. Vessels caught infringing the law were broken up. Transportation was brought in for almost anyone believed to be a smuggler who was carrying firearms or disguised in an attempt to avoid detection. Later the death penalty was imposed for assaulting preventive officers on duty and for bribing or attempting to bribe them. A convicted smuggler informing on his colleagues would be granted a free pardon. This made each smuggler suspicious of everyone else in the trade and led to intimidation and appalling violence and murder when reprisals were carried out. The death penalty was extended to include not just smuggling but assembling with the intention of running a contraband cargo and even harbouring smugglers on the run.

After the Napoleonic Wars ended in 1815, a more concerted and successful effort was made to counter the activities of the smugglers and this particular crime became less prevalent although it has never entirely died out.

Few items of potential contraband were as strange as the young woman who the disreputable rector of nearby Sneaton tried to have secretly carried aboard a Whitby coble, to be transferred to a local ship standing off-shore and then conveyed 'out of sight, out of mind' to London. She was his housekeeper, but their relationship had not been strictly professional and she had become pregnant. Anxious to avoid scandal and the cost of maintenance of the child, the rector has offered two coblemen a fair sum for the task. However, his reputation preceded him and they refused. This episode in 1702 landed the rector before a Consistory Court. There this fallen man of the cloth was described as 'a notorious drunkard and brawler'.

Scarborough was once a hive of smuggling activity. In 1768 three excise men stopped a cart lumbering along the road leading inland from Scarborough towards Malton. The two men with the cart escaped but not before one of the excise men was shot and fatally wounded. A generous reward was offered and the men, both locals, were captured and tried. The one who fired the shot was executed. The other was imprisoned at York Castle and there is no record of him being released. The load on the cart had included thirty half-ankers of gin and 240lbs of tea. The price such goods could fetch was enough to drive smugglers to murder and violence.

In the 1770s the local 'free trade' was dominated by a swaggering gangster called George 'Snooker' Fagg. He had a schooner *Kent* which was so heavily armed that it completely outmatched the local preventive vessels. In 1777, Fagg was off Filey when two preventive vessels called on him to heave to or risk being fired on. Fagg's defiant reply was, 'Fire away you buggers and be damned!' In fact, the smuggler for once was outgunned and his ship was badly damaged, but the wind dropped and the three vessels involved were virtually becalmed. Fagg placed his men in rowing boats and they then attempted to tow *Kent* away from danger. This enterprising effort was thwarted when two naval frigates appeared. The smugglers had no option but to surrender and they not only had to face the due process of the law but also the seizure of the contraband cargo of tea and spirits.

The use of payments for information about smuggling led to some particularly nasty scenes in 1822. In August 1822 several casks of smuggled gin were seized just to the north of

Scarborough but the smugglers evaded arrest. The preventive men offered a reward and Billy Mead from Burniston, just north of Scarborough, pointed the finger at James Law, a local wool merchant. Law (who certainly was a smuggler) strenuously denied Mead's accusation and eventually Mead was found guilty of perjury. The Scarborough smuggling fraternity decided to deter other would-be narks. A local man called Dobson had also given evidence against Law and he was set upon in the middle of Scarborough, being beaten up and severely injured and lucky to escape with his life. This episode had cheered the smugglers up and got them rather over-excited. In an advanced state of drunkenness, later in the evening, Law and some others made their way to Burniston and Billy Mead's house. They hurled insults at its occupant who replied by shooting into the darkness and succeeding, although entirely by chance, in hitting Law, who later died of his injuries. As might be expected, emotions were running high and other suspected informants were attacked. Mead was charged with murder and a local jury, likely to have sympathy with the smugglers, found him guilty. He went to prison.

Close to the harbour in Sandsend is the former Three Mariners inn, which was placed so that its patrons, who included a fair number of smugglers, had a fine view of all the comings and goings around the harbour including the activities of the local preventive service cutters. This is now a museum of smuggling.

Flamborough has a pub called the Rose and Crown which, in the 1840s, was used as a base for the illicit activities of the local smugglers. In 1844 a local lad called Jewison, in all innocence, stumbled on men moving kegs and casks around in the cellar, and a horse and cart outside with the horse's hooves and the cart's wheels muffled with rags. Being a bright spark he realised that smuggling was going on and that he might be in line for a reward if he informed the authorities. When approached by one of the smugglers, who advised him to keep quiet, he continued to use his brain and decided that silence was the order of the day. His discretion was rewarded when the smugglers dropped a tub of brandy off for his grandfather.

Nearby Flamborough Head has many caves, some of which are said to have been used as hidey-holes by the local smugglers. North Landing at Flamborough was notorious as a place where contraband came and went.

Bridlington was the scene of smuggling accurately recorded as early as 1278. Seven men, including the Prior of Bridlington, were implicated in smuggling large amounts of wool out of Filey. This 'smuggling in reverse' was known as 'owling' and was very common in the Middle Ages when there was a keen demand on the Continent for English raw wool and also finished cloth. The Crown levied duty on such exports and therefore smuggling became worthwhile.

In 1700 a local man was found guilty and imprisoned for exporting malt without paying duty. About the same time, the story is told that a ship came into Bridlington Harbour with its flag at half-mast and the crew came on shore behind six men bearing a coffin. The coffin contained tobacco and it was loaded onto a cart and wheeled through the streets, although not to any place of burial. Its contents were last heard of being sold in York.

The preventive men must have felt that their efforts went largely unappreciated by officialdom, especially if the paucity of resources that were provided was anything to go by. Their unpopularity in the community, their poor wages and under-funding made them vulnerable to bribery, particularly to turn a blind eye or to ensure that they were on urgent business elsewhere when a smuggling run was taking place. What comes as a surprise was the fact that,

The condemned cell in the Castle Prison at York. This housed many bounders in its day, including men who smuggled on the Yorkshire coast.

not only were there preventive men who could not be bought, but there were others who were injured or even killed bravely trying to enforce the law and often against overwhelming odds. Not all were so courageous, however. A newspaper report of 1821 described a Customs vessel which went to intercept a cutter suspected of smuggling in Bridlington Bay. Derisively the newspaper claimed that the Customs people backed off when they realised that all the crew of the cutter were over 6ft tall! Officialdom tried to scotch this story by claiming that the seas had been so rough at the time that the Customs vessel had been unable to get close enough to the cutter to see anyone on board, let alone to conclude that they were all of giant stature.

In 1750 information was received by the preventive men that a smuggling run was planned near Skipsea, which is situated on a lonely stretch of coast. A small force of men then turned up and spent two fruitless nights watching and waiting for a ship that never came. That is not quite right – it did come but several miles down the coast! Such experiences were common. From the point of view of the smugglers they served two purposes. They provided a diversion and meant that the coast was likely to be clear for a smuggling run elsewhere. They also annoyed the preventive men and used up their scarce resources.

Hornsea and indeed the Holderness district itself were ideal for smuggling purposes because of their remoteness and the ease of landing for illicit cargoes. Lonely sand dunes made convenient places for temporary storage of smuggled goods. The story is told that the parish clerk at Hornsea was an active smuggler back in 1732 and that he allowed the crypt of the parish church to be used for storing contraband. It was a cold and stormy December night when he was down in the crypt to check on the latest consignment of contraband. An exceptionally strong gust of wind destroyed much of the church roof, a sudden act of natural violence that shocked him so badly that he was struck dumb and daft. He died soon afterwards. Certain sanctimonious locals averred that this was God's punishment on the man for defiling the church by using it as a depot for smuggled goods.

14

THE PIERS OF YORKSHIRE

The seaside resorts of Britain trace their origins to the first half of the eighteenth century when a number of physicians, such as Sir John Floyer and Dr Richard Russell, began to recommend the health-giving virtues of inhaling ozone and bathing in and also drinking seawater. To do so, they asserted, was to help to cure an extremely diverse range of ailments and conditions which included rheumatism, cancer, hernias, deafness, ulcers, consumption and even infertility! People who lived near the sea had always liked a dip in the briny but now the well-to-do, especially that sizeable minority of them that were hypochondriacs, started making their way to seaside locations searching for not-too-demanding ways of restoring their health. Among the places that began to cater for this new clientele were Brighton, Margate and Scarborough.

To a large extent, but never totally, these seaside towns took over from the fashionable inland watering places or spas such as Bath or Tunbridge Wells. These had supposedly health-giving mineral waters and a sojourn there combined therapy and exercise with a range of congenial social activities, access to which had much to do with a visitor's social status and depth of pocket.

The problem was that inland transport in the period from 1750 to 1840 might have been somewhat better than it had been in the past but it was still, generally-speaking, tedious, expensive, inconvenient and sometimes hazardous. The preferred way of getting around Britain before the so-called 'Transport Revolution' was by water where possible. Not only does Britain have a fair number of rivers which could be navigated inland, sometimes for considerable distances, but she also had a very long coast in relation to her size and a tradition of going down to the sea in ships. Especially before railways began to probe into almost every corner of the United Kingdom, many passengers tried to reach these seaside places by sailing boat and, later, by steamship. However, few passengers enjoyed the uncomfortable and sometimes hazardous task of leaving the steamship offshore to transfer to a small, open rowing boat to be ferried to the shore at those resorts that did not have any suitable jetty or harbour – which was most of them.

What was more natural, therefore, than to build a landing stage for the pleasure boats carrying people to and from the resort? In 1814 Ryde, on the Isle of Wight, became possibly the first resort to build a wooden landing pier and nine years later the famous so-called 'Chain Pier' was opened at Brighton. This town was then at the height of its fashionable popularity. The new pier soon found itself not only being used for boarding and disembarking from pleasure ships but also as a place where people obtained pleasure from strolling in order to see others and, in turn, to be seen themselves. In other words, the Chain Pier doubled as a promenade with the added charm and not a little excitement that it was possible to walk over the waves. At the same time there were prospects of the town that could only be had from this novel location. All this and no danger of being seasick!

Further piers were built in small numbers between 1830 and 1860, by which time the railways had expanded into most parts of the kingdom. They enabled middle- and working-class people from inland towns to take advantage of cheap fares for visiting the seaside. For many of them this would have been the first time they had seen the sea. Day trips were most common at first and longer stays only became feasible with increases in real wages and later with the spread of holidays with pay. Those resorts that were easily reached by steamer, such as Margate and Southend, or by rail, such as Blackpool, Weston-super-Mare and Skegness, grew rapidly, largely as cheap and cheerful places for the urban masses. Most of them developed a range of similar amenities which included piers. Many of these piers serviced steamers plying to and from other resorts or centres of population, and they might also be the embarkation points for small boats providing trips around the bay or to local places of interest. Seaside resorts all felt that they ought to have piers and eventually most of them did.

Admission prices were usually charged for the public to have access to the piers. Pleasure-seekers, having paid the admission fee (which was often not cheap), felt that they should get a more all-round experience for their money. So a range of kiosks and stalls selling such things as novelties and souvenirs, candy floss, toffee apples and other eatables of dubious provenance began to appear along with fortune-tellers, mutoscopes or 'what-the-butler-saw' machines, bandstands, refreshment rooms and all the paraphernalia associated with the provision of commercialised pleasure.

Iron began to be used to replace wood in the construction of these piers, and improved methods of pile-driving and laying foundations added to the strength and stability of piers, some of which were becoming increasingly large. The first pier to be opened purely as a pleasure pier and not as a landing stage was almost certainly Southport Pier, which opened in 1860, constructed mainly of iron.

What might be described as a 'Pier Mania' then began and between 1860 and 1910 about ninety pleasure piers were built around the coasts of Britain and the Isle of Man, although very few opened in Scotland. Not all were successful. Speculators put up finance for them, as did small savers looking for a safe return, and both sometimes got their fingers burnt. Pier companies frequently used the powers of limited liability in order to attract investment but it has to be said that some piers, especially in the smaller resorts, never made a penny for their investors.

A few piers developed into what we might now call 'leisure centres' with a very wide range of amenities and amusements. Where they combined these with the facilities for handling steamers, they sometimes elicited complaints from local businessmen because trippers might arrive and spend their entire time on the pier rather than looking around the town and spending their money there. It didn't help that piers were often built and owned by companies based elsewhere.

Yorkshire's Piers

Yorkshire's long coastline had a number of developing resorts in the nineteenth century and was well to the fore where pier-building was concerned. A pier at Saltburn was mooted as early as 1861. It was eventually opened in 1869, followed by others at Scarborough (1869); Redcar (1873); Coatham (1875); Withernsea (1878) and Hornsea (1880). By 1910, four of these piers had been demolished. Many piers were short-lived; they were vulnerable to a range of hazards.

It will be noticed that Redcar and Scarborough were the only major resorts on the Yorkshire coast to acquire pleasure piers. Filey, Whitby and Bridlington did without them. The last two had existing stone harbour walls and jetties which could be used for promenading. The other places with pleasure piers were very much minor resorts with limited commercial appeal and this was reflected in the piers that were built.

One problem was that the major Yorkshire resorts, that is, Redcar, Whitby, Scarborough, Filey and Bridlington, were all rather distant from the places where most of their visitors lived. Blackpool was always Britain's premier working-class resort and it creamed off a lot of the potential business from Yorkshire. So too did Morecambe, which was sometimes called 'Bradford-on-Sea'. Southport and New Brighton were other resorts in the north-west with easier access to and from their hinterlands. Large numbers may have converged on Scarborough and Bridlington in particular, but some of the west coast resorts were better located and equipped to develop their leisure business on a mass, in fact industrial, scale.

Leaving social and economic concerns aside, it was the forces of nature that were largely to account for the disappearance of Yorkshire's piers. Scarborough Pier was so badly damaged in a severe storm in 1905 that it was never rebuilt. Three others were damaged beyond economic repair by sailing ships. These were difficult to control in stormy weather and heavy seas and seemed remarkably prone to colliding with piers. Hornsea Pier had only been open for five months when, during a storm, it was hit by a ship which wrecked the pierhead and brought down about 120ft of the structure. The pier company, already in dire financial straits, simply could not afford to repair it and the wreckage was left to rot. Withernsea Pier seemed to attract ships out of control like moths to a flame. It was smashed into and damaged so frequently that eventually there was virtually nothing left for any ship to damage. Coatham Pier was a quite impressive structure but simply too near its rival at Redcar and the two adjacent resorts could not drum up enough trade to make two piers pay. In 1898 Coatham Pier was neatly cut in two when a ship went into it. The pier company went bust and the remains of the pier were scrapped. Redcar Pier, by contrast, managed to survive until 1981. The last surviving Yorkshire pleasure pier, at Saltburn, was almost demolished in 1974 following several chequered decades. A public enquiry was held and in 1978 it was slightly reduced in length, restored and reopened.

Saltburn Pier was a fairly standard structure consisting of cast-iron piles supporting trestles also of cast-iron which in turn supported the wooden decking. It was 1,500ft long, 20ft wide and had a landing stage at the further end used largely by pleasure steamers. Two octagonal kiosks were placed at the pier entrance for use as tollhouses, and facilities on the pier included a saloon bar and refreshment booths. This pier opened in 1869 and was immediately successful; around 50,000 holiday-makers paid to use it in the first six months. Pleasure steamers plied their trade to and from Hartlepool, Whitby, Scarborough and Bridlington and these trips proved to be very popular. This success was not sustained, and profits were falling when in 1875 a storm caused severe damage. The pier company went bust and the Saltburn Improvement Company took over in 1883 and effected many improvements. The pier, with its fishing, its band concerts and its promenading, was the major attraction in the town. A tramway was built up the cliff to improve access to and from the town centre.

In 1924, a ship carrying china clay from Fowey in Cornwall to Grangemouth in Scotland hit the pier and brought a large section down which was not rebuilt until 1930. In 1938 the local authority took the pier over. In 1940 it was requisitioned by the Army who removed a long section to prevent its possible use as a landing point by the Germans.

Post-war, the pier was in poor condition but it was repaired and reopened in 1952, only to be battered by storms a few months later and then closed until 1958. In that year its popularity can be measured by the fact that 90,000 people used it. By the 1970s it was evident that severe metal corrosion had taken place and that the structure was becoming unsafe. In 1973 it was only open in calm weather. Storms inflicted considerable damage in 1974 and the local authority, as owner, applied for planning permission to demolish the pier and rid itself of a serious financial liability. The upshot was that permission was refused and very extensive repairs and refurbishment took place. Money has continued to be spent to ensure that this, the sole survivor of Yorkshire's pleasure piers, can be enjoyed by future generations.

Like other Yorkshire piers, that at Saltburn-on-Sea has undergone many vicissitudes but has survived and is a delightful structure redolent of the heyday of the Victorian resort.

Let's have a quick look at the fate of the other Yorkshire piers. The first proposal to build a pier at Scarborough was in 1864 and this would have been close to the harbour. This scheme came to nothing because it was thought that such a pier might endanger shipping movements. In 1865 a local banker formed a company to build a 1,000ft-long pier in the underdeveloped North Bay area of the town. He engaged the celebrated pier designer Eugenius Birch as engineer and in 1869 the pier opened, having cost £12,135 to build. Entrance fee was a penny and an annual ticket to allow access for fishing could be had for just £1. The pier had cost more to build than had been budgeted for and turned out to be a white elephant. It was hoped that steamers would call, bringing much-needed revenue, but the first two or three that did call hit the pier and damaged both themselves and the pier so further visits by such vessels were vetoed. Storm damage was constant and by 1879 the pier had ceased to make money while the cost of repairs was mounting. Two ships crashed into the pier on separate occasions in 1883. A cliff tramway that had been built in association with the pier closed down and the owners decided to put the pier up for sale. Surprisingly, perhaps, it was bought by a London-based company who spent a lot on repairs and improvements, encouraged by the opening up of the Royal Albert Drive which linked the North and South Bays. Scarborough Pier seemed fated, however, and it continued its history of losing money until the exceptionally stormy night of 6 January 1905 when it was battered to pieces. It had not been insured and this marked the end for Scarborough Pier, the last traces being removed in 1914.

The Redcar Pier Company was established in 1866 but soon ran into problems when next-door Coatham also proposed the building of a pier. A compromise to build just one pier midway between the two places could not be reached and so work started in 1871, the official opening being in 1873. The pier was 1,300ft long and at the pierhead there was a sheltered bandstand with 700 seats. Steamers plied to and from Middlesbrough, Saltburn and Whitby. Redcar suffered from what seemed to be the occupational hazards of Yorkshire piers: storms and ships out of control. In 1880 and 1885 the pier was breached by ships, and steamers were no longer allowed to call. In 1897 another wrecked ship hit the pier and in 1898 the pierhead suffered a severe fire. In 1907 a plush ballroom was built at the shore end but the condition deteriorated over the years. In the Second World War a floating mine exploded nearby, inflicting further damage, and storms removed most of what was by now a very rickety structure. When the war ended, just the pier pavilion and 45ft of the neck remained. By now this was the shortest pier in Britain and something of a joke, but even its now diminutive size did not prevent it from sustaining further storm damage, especially in 1953, and it closed to the public as unsafe in 1980. Eventually all that was left was the ballroom in which a mighty Wurlitzer organ had been installed in 1979. Ironically, in its last couple of years the pier had seemed to be more popular than ever before. No money was available for rebuilding and demolition of what was left took place by March 1981.

A proposal to build a pier at Coatham was first heard of in 1870. Work started in 1873 and the pier at 2,000ft was to be 700ft longer than its hated rival at Redcar which was already open. In 1874 it was almost complete when it was hit within minutes of each other by a brig and then a schooner, both out of control during a storm. The structure was partly destroyed and the length reduced to 1,800ft when it was opened in 1875. It possessed two pavilions, one of which had an ice-skating rink. Coatham Pier lasted for only about twenty-four years, never making significant money for its owners, and in 1898 it was severely damaged by a Finnish sailing vessel. The cost of repairs was prohibitive and the pier was demolished in 1899, although the pavilions survived until 1910.

Work on building the pier at Withernsea began in 1875 and even before it was complete it suffered storm damage. It was 1,196ft long and was finished and opened to the public in 1878. Its most distinctive features were two brick-built and castellated gateways which soon became affectionately – or mockingly – known as 'The Sandcastle'. Someone who claimed that they were designed to resemble Conwy Castle in North Wales had clearly never seen the latter. The pier was moderately successful but, in a massive storm in 1880, it was hit by two sailing ships which caused considerable damage. Repairs took place but storms inflicted more damage in 1882. This time it was not repaired but it stayed open and people entered the pier at their own risk. In 1890 a Grimsby fishing smack hit the pier and brought much of the somewhat rickety structure down. In 1893 yet another vessel hit what was left of the pier. With the exception of 'The Sandcastle', the sad remnants were removed in 1903. 'The Sandcastle' is still there, now generally referred to just as 'The Castle'.

Hornsea Pier was authorised in 1876 as part of an ambitious plan for a whole new town including a tramway from the railway station to the pier. The speculators had been carried away. Then a rival pier was authorised! This, in a town well off the beaten track and with a population of just 1,600! In the event just one pier was built, designed by our friend Eugenius Birch, and it opened in 1880 having already provided financial problems for its promoters. It was 1,072ft long. It attracted most of the people who came to visit Hornsea because quite frankly there wasn't much else there, but its career was a short one. The same terrific storm in October 1880 that badly damaged Redcar and Withernsea Piers launched a vessel named *The Earl of Derby* straight into Hornsea's pier. The pier was severely damaged and taken out of public use. It was reported derelict in 1897 and was an eyesore until most of it was demolished in 1910. A few fragments were visible as late as 1929.

15

THE RAILWAYS OF SCARBOROUGH AND WHITBY

Scarborough's rise from a small fishing port via a select watering place to a major holiday resort was greatly facilitated by the coming of the railways. The line built from York by the York & North Midland Railway, which opened in 1845, was the brainchild of George Hudson, then approaching the peak of his powers as a railway promoter and manager. Not everyone in Scarborough welcomed the railway and a local man gave voice to these concerns in a pamphlet when he wrote that the town had …

> …no wish for a greater influx of vagrants, and those who have no money to spend. Scarborough is rising daily in the estimation of the fashionable as a watering place on account of its natural beauty and tranquillity and in a few more years the novelty of not having a railroad will be its greatest asset'.

His profound misunderstanding of the impact of the railways counted for little and Scarborough began to flourish as never before as a holiday resort for middle-class and better-off working-class visitors who almost all came by rail. Something which must have been even more anathema to our misanthropic friend was the cheap railway excursion train. The first of these was from Newcastle-on-Tyne and it arrived at Scarborough less than a month after the railway opened. The excursionists must have been made of stern stuff because the 250-mile round trip was in open-top carriages. For the majority of them, however, this would have been the most exciting day of their lives – as adventurous almost as a trip to the moon.

Scarborough probably enjoyed its peak years as a popular resort in the 1930s, and it is difficult for us to grasp just how many people would arrive in the town by rail on a summer Saturday before the onset of generalised car ownership. On August Bank Holiday Saturday 1939, 102 main-line trains arrived and 106 departed between 5.07 in the morning and 11.45 at night. This total does not include local trains to such places as Hull and Whitby. Regular Saturdays-only trains arrived brim-full of holiday-makers from such places as London, Birmingham, Glasgow,

Manchester and Nottingham. Included in the total are day excursions, particularly from places in South and West Yorkshire and Tyneside.

Scarborough station was on an extremely lavish scale for a town of its size. It once had as many platforms as King's Cross and even those were not enough, so an overspill station had to be opened at Londesborough Road. The frontage of Scarborough station is adorned by a rather attractive clock tower erected in 1884. This was built as the result of an agreement between the North Eastern Railway, which then controlled all the railways serving Scarborough, and the town council. The latter agreed to pay for the gas needed to illuminate the clock at night if the North Eastern Railway provided a clock capable of being illuminated. The station is now a Grade I listed building.

Another type of special train run particularly in the 1930s was the 'evening excursion'. These trains mostly came from big towns in the West Riding such as Leeds, Wakefield and Bradford and would arrive between 6 p.m. and 7.30 in the evening. They would leave between 10.15 and 11.25. The first to arrive were also the first to leave. They allowed people living well inland three or more hours by the sea in the evening. Some happy excursionists got off the train at Scarborough and got no further than the pub nearest to the railway station. Obviously then the idea was to sink as many pints as possible and make sure they did not miss the train back. Many of them did. These trains were often composed of ancient compartment carriages without corridors or toilets. It was usually a run of at least two hours home by which time bladders must have been at bursting point.

Messrs Bass, Ratcliffe & Gretton were the largest brewing company in Burton-on-Trent. Just as Manchester was sometimes called 'Cottonopolis' and Bradford 'Worstedopolis', so Burton could have been nicknamed 'Beeropolis'. The town was totally dominated by the production of beer. In 1865 the company started running a free railway day excursion in the summer for its employees and their relations and friends. Between 1865 and 1883 these trains ran biennially, but from that year they became an annual event right up to and including 1914. Scarborough was the destination in 1881, 1890, 1894, 1898, 1902, 1906, 1910 and 1914. Six trains were run on 17 June 1881 carrying 3,500 pleasure-seekers and the peak was reached in 1898 with no fewer than fifteen trains carrying 9,000 excursionists.

Taking the first Bass excursion to Scarborough as an example, the earliest train left Burton at 4 a.m., arriving in Scarborough at 8.40. The other trains followed at ten minute intervals. The trippers were all issued with a free ticket for dinner at the Scarborough Aquarium. Each sitting catered for about 300 and between them the trippers consumed 3,750lbs of beef, 6,000 dinner rolls, 24 gallons of pickles, 72 bottles of Worcester Sauce and a 1,000 veal and ham pies. Male employees were given a shilling and a day's wages and boys received sixpence plus wages. They were given free admission to a special selection of entertainments at the Aquarium and the spa and a free ride on the South Cliff tramway. The first train left for Burton at 6.10 p.m. and the last got back to that town at 12.50 a.m.

Clearly this cost Bass & Co. a large amount of money but it was seen as a highly worthwhile investment. It provided advertising because the media of the day were fascinated by the event and gave it free publicity. It was also thought to encourage loyalty among the employees and discourage strikes with their consequent loss of production. The traders and licensees of Scarborough were all in favour because 3,500 excursionists represented a lot of spending power.

The organisation of these excursions was carried out with military precision and the accommodation in the trains for employees, and those travelling with them, was strictly demarcated according to the status of each worker. Everyone was issued with a very strict set of rules about how to behave and what to do and what not to do. Every excursionist was also issued with a commemorative brochure containing a résumé of the history of Scarborough and a guide to the resort's attractions and amenities, plus a further set of dos and don'ts and numerous reminders about the company's generosity.

The journey from Burton was 136 miles and it included a refreshment halt and comfort break at York. As might be expected, there was a huge rush for the toilets and for tea, so much so that in 1910 trippers cleaned out the entire supply of cups and saucers from the York refreshment rooms. Trippers were instructed to place the crockery on the luggage racks in their compartments, allowing them to be rounded up and returned later.

The most spectacular railway serving Scarborough, and indeed one of the most scenic railways in the whole of England, was that which ran from Scarborough to Whitby via Hayburn Wyke, Ravenscar and Robin Hood's Bay and then on, hugging the cliffs from Whitby through Sandsend, Kettleness and Staithes and eventually to Middlesbrough.

The Scarborough & Whitby Railway was opened in 1885 and soon became part of the North Eastern Railway. At Whitby it crossed the valley of the Esk on the spectacular Larpool Viaduct which was 915ft long. It now carries a footpath and cycle track and affords breathtaking views of the Esk Valley. It looks positively awesome from below. The line was remarkable for its ferocious gradients, especially those of 1 in 39 and 1 in 41 at Ravenscar. This is very steep by railway standards and the difficulties of operation were greatly increased by mists rolling in off the sea which made the rails greasy. A guide published around the time the line opened had this to say about the line's delights:

> The line has opened out the country and made it accessible in all its virgin loveliness. The line runs through pleasant undulating pasture lands at either end, winds in and out among the gorse and heatherclad hills, dips into wooded dales, skirts the edge of a wild moor, climbs the highest cliff on the Yorkshire coast, runs round one of the bonniest bays in the Kingdom, and over a portion of its course is perched on the brow of a cliff against which the waves ceaselessly break.

Intermediate stations on this line were at Scalby, Cloughton, Hayburn Wyke, Staintondale, Ravenscar and Robin Hood's Bay, after which they ran into the West Cliff station at Whitby, the main building of which still exists. Camping coaches were a feature of this line and of the route further up the coast from Whitby. These could be hired as holiday accommodation and were parked in sidings close to stations having a picturesque position. One condition of hiring the accommodation was that users had to travel by train. Examples of stations with camping coaches on this line were Stainton Dale and Ravenscar.

The line between Scarborough and Whitby closed in 1965 after loud protests. That between Whitby and Loftus had closed in 1958. It was apparent then, and remains so, that these closures were a mistake. On bad winters the roads could become impassable because of snow but the railways rarely did. The views that could be had in fine weather, such as those between Kettleness, Sandsend

Larpool Viaduct. This spectacular viaduct carried the Whitby to Scarborough railway across the deep valley of the River Esk just inland from Whitby.

and Whitby, and from Robin Hood's Bay to Ravenscar, were second to none on England's railways. The Scarborough to Whitby line would probably now be a major tourist attraction, especially if it could have linked up with the main line system at Scarborough and Whitby and had a link to the North Yorkshire Moors Railway. It could have helped to reduce traffic congestion and the carbon footprint, not that that particular phrase was in use in 1965. It is too late now.

Northwards up the coast from Whitby, the line was if anything even more spectacular. It was opened by the North Eastern Railway in the 1880s. The best-known features were five spindly-looking viaducts on tubular metal columns. The largest was at Staithes and it was unique because it had a wind-gauge attached to it. The viaduct was exceptionally exposed and the idea was that the wind-gauge would be activated when the wind reached the velocity at which it would be unsafe for trains to run over it. A bell would then alert the signalman, who would put all his signals at danger and stop the trains. The problem was that the apparatus was sometimes faulty and the bell might sound in the signal box when there wasn't as much as a zephyr of wind, and remain totally silent when a near hurricane-force wind was coming off the North Sea. The unreliability of this apparatus was such that on a particularly rough night, the driver of a train going south stopped at Grinkle and rang up the Staithes signalman to ask if the bell was sounding. When the signalman told him it wasn't, the driver replied that it bloody-well should be. Undaunted, he then drove the train across the viaduct so fast that it rushed straight through Staithes station where it was supposed to stop. It then had to reverse. The line was closed in 1958 and all the viaducts were subsequently demolished in 1958, but a few traces of their piers can still be seen.

A Standard 2-6-4T crossing Staithes Viaduct with a train from Whitby, probably destined for Middlesbrough. This viaduct was opened in 1883.

Whitby West Cliff railway station. The main buildings of the old West Cliff station at Whitby can still be seen, now converted to housing, but there is very little evidence that trains ever ran here.

Going north from Whitby there were stations at Sandsend, Kettleness, Hinderwell, Staithes, Grinkle and then Loftus. Sandsend and Staithes were two that had camping coaches. Most trains on this stretch of line worked through from Scarborough and Whitby to Middlesbrough via Guisborough. No one would argue that the lines between Scarborough and Whitby, and up the coast to Loftus, traversed fairly sparsely populated country with little originating passenger traffic and probably even less goods and minerals. Given the terrain through which they ran, they had been expensive to build and were also obviously expensive to maintain. Their decline and disappearance, however, were the result of generations of politicians who proved totally incapable of providing the country with a coherent policy towards transport.

Scarborough is currently served by trains to York, most of which continue to Leeds, Huddersfield, Manchester and Liverpool. There is a not particularly frequent service southwards to Filey, Bridlington and Hull. Whitby has a very sparse service along the Esk Valley to Middlesbrough. It travels through some extraordinarily beautiful countryside but unfortunately this means that it is neither easy, quick nor convenient to get to Whitby by train via this route.

16

SOME PLACE NAMES OF THE YORKSHIRE COAST

It might be helpful to take a quick look at some of the place names on and around this coastline to see what light they shed on its history. The elements of the place names are given and an explanation of what these elements mean, with their linguistic origin, and then one or more examples:

-burn: This means spring or stream and comes from Saxon. Examples are Saltburn and Sherburn near Filey.

-bury, burgh, borough: This means fortified place and comes from Saxon. The prime example is of course Scarborough, which according to legend was the fortified place built by a fellow called Skarthi whose name meant 'hare-lipped'. Some argue that the name is Norse in origin and comes from 'skarth-berg' meaning 'gap hill' since the town lies between two cliffs. In the twelfth century the name of the town is recorded as being 'Escardeburg'. Similar are Flamborough and Goldsborough, north of Whitby.

-by: This is extremely common as a place name ending, particularly in the north and east of England. It means farmstead, village or small settlement and is a word of Norse origin. Whitby is a good example. There are two opinions on this one. Some say it was 'hwit-by' meaning 'white village', but the general opinion is that it was from a personal name – Hviti, perhaps. It was Witebi in Domesday and Quiteby in 1219. Other similar names include Hunmanby, Scalby, Osgodby and Carnaby and there is the wonderful Ugglebarnby outside Whitby.

-clough (or sometimes as a prefix): This means ravine or deep valley and is a Saxon word. An example is Cloughton just north of Scarborough.

-cot, -cote or -coton: These mean cottage, shelter or hut and are of Saxon derivation. Not many in this area but perhaps Cottingham, north of Hull.

-ea, -ey: A little confusion here because '-ea' normally refers to a small river or stream while '-ea' and '-ey' can be an island. Both are of Saxon origin. Skipsea, Hornsea, Kilnsea and Withernsea provide examples.

-ham: This means a homestead or village and is Saxon. Examples include: Kilham near Driffield, Levisham near Pickering, Coatham near Redcar and Wykeham near Scarborough.

-haugh: Meaning enclosure or fenced land, this stem is Nordic. There aren't many in this area but Salthaugh Grange near Hedon is an example.

-holm and -holme: Meaning small island or sometimes meadow, this is Norse or Danish in origin. Examples are Lealholm near Whitby, Waxholme near Withernsea and Holme on the Wolds.

-ing, -ings: This means people of or belonging to. It has Saxon roots. Bridlington probably means the farmstead belonging to Beorhtel, a Saxon gentleman. Other examples include Patrington, Ottrington and Skinningrove.

-ness: A Saxon and a Norse stem. In the first case it means headland and in the second, copse. There is the hamlet of Kettleness up the coast from Whitby, a Scalby Ness and a Ness Point near Robin Hood's Bay. 'Ness Point' is a bit of a tautology.

-thorpe, -thorp: This means minor settlement or farm, is of Nordic or Saxon origin and extremely common in this part of the country. Fylingthorpe, Hilderthorpe and Lowthorpe provide examples.

-ton: This means farmstead, enclosure or manor and is derived from Saxon. One of the most common name-place elements, this can be found, for example, at Patrington, Lockington, Bridlington, Burniston, Bempton and Brotton.

-wyke: This comes from the medieval English 'wic' which means 'dairy farm'. Alternatively it can denote a bay or creek. Wyke Hole between Whitby and Scarborough is an example; another is Hayburn Wyke, north of Scarborough.

Below are some individual place names from north to south with definition, language of origin and probable first mention.

Middlesbrough: 'Middlemost stronghold'; Old English, i.e. around AD 400–1150; *c.* 1165.

Redcar: 'Red or reedy marsh'; Old English or Old Scandinavian, i.e. Viking origin; *c.* 1170.

Marske-by-the-Sea: 'Place by a marsh'; Old English; *c.* 1086.

Saltburn-by-the-Sea: 'Place near a salty stream' Old English; 1185.

Staithes: 'Landing-place'; Old English; not known.

Hinderwell: Probably 'a spring or well associated with St Hild'; perhaps both Old English and Old Scandinavian; not known.

Runswick Bay: Possibly something like 'creek or inlet belonging to Reinn'; Old Scandinavian; *c.* 1273.

High Hawsker: 'Enclosure belonging to Haukr'; Old Scandinavian; *c.* 1125.

Cayton: 'farmstead belonging to Caega'; Old English; 1086.

Filey: Possibly a reference to Filey Brigg and meaning 'headland shaped like a sea monster' or possibly 'place near five clearings'; Both are Old English; 1086.

Mappleton: 'Farmstead with maple trees'; Old English; 1086.

Withernsea: Could be 'lake or watery place near a thorn tree'; Old English: 1086.

Spurn Head: From 'a projecting piece of land'; Middle English, i.e. 1100–1500; 1399.

Thorngumbald: 'Close to a thorn tree'; Old English; 1086.

Hedon: 'Hill where heather grows'; Old English; twelfth century.

Other titles published by The History Press

East Yorkshire Curiosities
ROBERT WOODHOUSE

This book is a guide to the remarkable and curious sights to be found in East Yorkshire. Featured here are buildings, bear pits, cemeteries, castles and follies, memorials, tramways and inns, whose strange histories are explained by author Robert Woodhouse. There are numerous illustrations, together with location and access details for each site, allowing readers to discover an immense variety of history, humanity and architecture for themselves

978 0 7524 5619 5

Haunted Whitby
ALAN BROOKE

With stories of haunted lighthouses, creepy tunnels, a haunted silk shawl, goblins, the strange apparitions of Bagdale Hall, the spirit of Nunnington Hall and the ghosts of smugglers from shipwrecks, and illustrated with over sixty chilling photographs, *Haunted Whitby* is a must-read for anyone interested in the town's paranormal past.

978 0 7524 4925 8

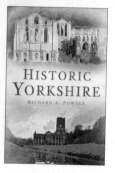

Historic Yorkshire
RICHARD A. POWELL

This volume celebrates every aspect of Yorkshire's history. Including subjects as diverse as Roman Yorkshire, Yorkshire castles and abbeys, historic York, prehistoric Yorkshire, Yorkshire folklore, Robin Hood of Yorkshire, ghost houses, industry, canals and railways, it is a fascinating tour through Yorkshire's past. Richly illustrated and meticulously researched, this book will delight all lovers of the Dales.

978 0 7524 4926 5

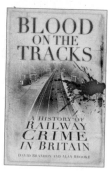

Blood on the Tracks: A History of Railway Crime in Britain
DAVID BRANDON AND ALAN BROOKE

This fascinating history covers all varieties of crime on the railways and how it has changed over the years, from assaults and robberies, to theft of goods, murder, vandalism, football and other crowd activity, suicide on the line, fraud and white-collar crime, and also looks at the use of railway crime in film and literature.

978 0 7524 5231 9

Visit our website and discover thousands of other History Press books.

www.thehistorypress.co.uk